PAR
MATC

FALLING IN (
WITH THE FR

PARIS MATCH

FALLING IN (LOVE)
WITH THE FRENCH

John von Sothen

PROFILE BOOKS

First published in Great Britain in 2020 by

Profile Books
29 Cloth Fair, Barbican, London EC1A 7JQ.

www.profilebooks.com

An earlier version of this book was published as
Monsieur Mediocre by Viking Penguin in the US (2019).

1 3 5 7 9 10 8 6 4 2

Typeset in Sina
to a design by Henry Iles.

A CIP catalogue record for this book is available from the
British Library.

ISBN 978-1788164597
e-ISBN 978-1782836582

Printed and bound in Great Britain by Clays Ltd, Elcograf S.p.A.
on Forest Stewardship Council (mixed sources) certified paper.

To the Annes in my life

My mother, Annie-Lou, who brought me into this world

My wife, Anaïs, who helped me become a man

My editor, Anne Boulay, who let me write the way I am

CONTENTS

CONTENTS

CHAPTER ONE

SHE HAD ME
AT *BAH*

THE MOMENT I REALISED I deeply wanted to marry Anaïs was the moment when she casually reminded me that we could always get divorced. She said it in that French nonchalant way, preceding it with the classic '*Bah* ...' opener I've heard millions of times from her since. Anything following *bah* is blatantly obvious to the person saying it; the tone contains a mounting exasperation with the one hearing it, who is usually me: '*Bah* ... the drawer over there. Where else would we keep the batteries?' '*Bah* ... Gene Hackman, John. Who did you think I was talking about?'

I've always wanted to film Anaïs when she starts her *bahs*, then splice them together into one fluid *bah*, which I could then post online to show the world I married a woman who's part French lamb. In this case, Anaïs's *bah* was followed by the revelation that marriage wasn't the be-all and end-all I'd built it up in my head to be. She loved me, yes, and sure, we should try it, but if it didn't work out, '*Bah* ... we get divorced. What do you want me to say?'

At the time, we were standing on the medieval Pont-Neuf, the oldest bridge in Paris, which crosses the Seine and links the Left Bank with the Samaritaine department store on the right. The Pont-Neuf is one of those places in Paris that's so picturesque, you not only feel you're on a movie set when you're there, you're tempted to act out the film you think is being shot. It's been the backdrop for countless films, including the 1990s cult classic starring Juliette Binoche titled (not too ironically) *Les Amants du Pont-Neuf.*

Perhaps those walking past us that night felt the cinematic magic of the moment in that same 'Paris is for lovers' way. Anaïs and I were just another passionate couple caught up in the throes of romance. They expected us to embrace at any moment with a Bacall–Bogart kiss, and then attach a stupid lock to a nearby railing.

If anyone had overheard Anaïs, it might have ruined their moment. But, for me, it was an epiphany. She was right. We could always just get divorced. There was a fallback plan. All of a sudden, the pressure was off, so what was I waiting for? I kissed her then, realising no American woman I knew would ever have said that. Paris was my kind of town, cold and cynical, and Anaïs is as Parisian as they get.

Before this moment, I'd fallen in love with France through another woman, my mother, who'd lived in Paris for a year, in 1953, learning to paint at Les Beaux-Arts after she'd graduated from Vassar.

I know the date because I found among her belongings a dog-eared clipping taken from the Pittsburgh Press's society section, which detailed Mom's scheduled trip to Paris, where 'cobblestone streets, art galleries and the picturesqueness of French life are luring this young Miss'. The piece was accompanied by a photo of Mom painting on the front porch of her family's farmhouse outside Pittsburgh, and went on to announce she and my grandmother would be hosting a picnic later that week, and that both would be 'judging hats'.

As a child I'd listen to Mom's stories of France, snuggled into the nook of her neck, as we lay in her bed, she either reading aloud from a diary she'd kept during that year or staring at the ceiling and delivering the lines from memory, sometimes even in French. Often she'd start at the very beginning of her adventure on a slow steamer bound for Le Havre, during which she attended lavish dinners and dances, had drinks with Princeton boys, met a swarthy count from Montenegro and visited a tiger in steerage. Other times, she'd skip ahead and place us smack dab in the centre of Paris where she bunked with others in a tiny flat on the Île Saint-Louis, soaking up the free-spirit life of post-war Paris.

I knew these Paris characters by heart: Mimi, Mom's roommate, who convinced her to captain a canoe on the Seine with two bottles of wine, which led to their capsising and being fished out by the gendarmes. Or her starving art-ist friend, Hannah, who ate only onions because she want-ed to save money, and eating a raw onion apparently cuts your appetite. Then there was the struggling writer who had the unfortunate curse of sharing the last name Hemingway. 'Je me suis dit,' Mom declared in French, 'a famous writing career was not in the cards for Russell Hemingway.'

While she spoke, my mother would take on an exotic glow, as if she was inhabited by the actress Simone Signoret, and because I was keen on following each of her stories and descriptions, I'd latch on to certain words and phrases I knew as a way to cross the stream that was the rest of her *vouloir courir comme ça* French. During these nights *au lit*, me drifting off to sleep under France's fairytale spell, I imagined it as a land full of wonderment, taste and refinement, a place where Mom once shone, and where, one day, maybe I could, too.

Although the setting was perfect, Anaïs's and my timing was ass backwards. Normal couples fret about whether or not they should get married before one of them is pregnant. Not us. For Anaïs, the decision to have a child with me far outweighed whether we got married. Her friends were already having children with people they weren't married to and I'd met some of them, the woman usually referring to the silent man standing next to her not as her boyfriend or husband, but *le père de mon enfant* – 'the father of my child'.

Whereas my fellow Americans were doubling down on marriage in response to their divorce-addled parents, the French, it seemed, were headed in the other direction, abandoning the institution altogether or choosing from a sort of drive-thru menu of different options the French state offers. They had *mariage blanc* for people marrying to get green cards. There was something called PACS, a sort of common-law union for people who want the tax write-off, but who don't really believe in marriage. (Gay marriage was brought into law in 2012, but a lot of gay couples still use PACS because they think gay marriage is too hetero.) You could even live in something called *concubinage* (yes, you read that right – concublines are de facto couples living in what used to be called sin). And, if you do get married the traditional way, there's *mariage avec séparation de biens,* a pre-nup clause for the middle classes, found in any standard marriage contract, which ensures that whatever was yours before the marriage (apartments, juicers, ironically purchased vinyl records) is returned to you if the marriage expires.

All in all, the French have almost as many choices of marriage as they do cheese, which I guess is why it takes them so long to decide. Often marriage takes a backseat to the really big benchmarks in life, like having kids or buying a house. It's not odd to see a ten-year-old daughter carrying her mom's dress or little boys bringing the ring to their dad at a wedding. Or a *famille recomposée*, where both partners bring their kids and exes from the first and second marriages to the wedding. The French don't treat marriage as the start of some grand adventure as Americans do. It is more the 'we might as well get married now that we've done everything else' cherry on top. Marriages in France are for forty-year-olds who want to have a big party before their parents die.

A lot of this explained Anaïs's jaded response that night on the Pont-Neuf. That and the fact she'd already been married once. I hadn't, though, and expected to have much more clarity by this point, the kind that's supposed to hit you as you stand on a Parisian bridge on a warm night overlooking the Seine with the woman you love.

Up until our decision that night on the Pont-Neuf, my life had been a relatively idle and fancy-free one. I was living in New York, or more precisely Brooklyn, a freelance writer, single, and tethered to the city only by my membership to the NY Sports Club. On the ground floor of my building was a French café called Le Gamin. And it was there that I met my future wife.

Anaïs had one of those bobs with concave bangs French women seem to master, which make them look like adorable 1960s KGB agents. We'd chat over countless *cafés*, sometimes in French, sometimes in English – me never knowing where I really stood, because French women don't show their cards early. But all became clear when I one day offered her the ultimate gift, one no Parisian woman in the late 1990s could refuse – a biography of the Hong Kong film director Wong Kar-wai. It was a cheap ploy, since I knew Anaïs wasn't just a waitress, but an actress as well. For one of our first dates, she took me to a festival where a film she'd starred in was premiering. I'd never been somebody's arm candy before, so I relished the chance, only to find out moments later, when the lights dimmed and the film started rolling, that the Anaïs on screen was a deeply troubled person who slept with everyone, men and women alike.

My parents missed that movie, thank goodness, but were determined to meet Anaïs. They used the excuse of my thirtieth birthday to make a trip north from DC and drop by semi-unannounced, calling me on a Saturday morning to tell me they were on their way over for brunch.

After I hung up, my first instinct wasn't to cheerfully tell Anaïs that my parents were in town. It was to hide her or at least get her out of my apartment.

'They can't see you here!' I told her in a panicked voice.

Anaïs didn't understand. Instead, she squinted at me. (Just as I now find myself squinting on countless occasions in France when I find myself clueless.)

'Because they'll have the impression we're *sleeping* together.'
My tone was bitchy because all of this was so very obvious.

'Well, we are.'

'Yeah, but they don't know that.'

Anaïs then laughed in my face.

What I hadn't explained was that my parents were notoriously old. They'd been old since I was little. My dad had fought in World War II, and my mother had an *I like Ike* pin and drank gin and tonics.

They'd met in 1960s Washington, where my father, a perennial bachelor into his mid-forties, worked for the NBC affiliate WRC. Dad called himself a newsman, and for decades he was on the radio and TV, hosting a political round-table show called *Dimension Washington* or, as he liked to call it, *Dementia Washington*. He'd go on to win Emmy Awards for his work, one for a film titled *The Last Out*, a documentary about Griffith Stadium, the famed ballpark of the Washington Senators, which Dad argued was one of the last points of common ground for a city gradually becoming splintered.

My mother had become a full- time painter by then, making sketches of the people and places she encountered, drawings she called her 'charcoals', which she'd later transform into acrylic and oil canvases. These soon numbered into the hundreds, something she said was both a blessing and a curse: 'I had tons of paintings to hang, but no walls!'

The solution would come in the form of my father, who'd recently purchased a decrepit brownstone in the Georgetown neighbourhood of Washington. While many of his friends begged him to move to the suburbs after the riots in the 1960s, Dad doubled down on the city, buying this four-storey fixer-upper, which was weird, considering he lived alone. Weirder, my mother said, was when she visited the house for the first time and saw he'd only renovated a kitchen, a bathroom and part of a bedroom. The rest of the house was vacant.

The two had been set up through Dad's best friend, Mac McGarry, who as well as having the best name for TV hosted a weekly show at WRC called *It's Academic*, a sort of American *University Challenge* for high school students, which now resides in the *Guinness Book of World Records* as the longest-running quiz programme in TV history. Mac and his wife, Babette, had been trying unsuccessfully for years to set my father up. Then one New Year's Eve, a neighbour mentioned in passing that a young woman named Annie-Lou from Pittsburgh had just arrived and needed a last-minute date. They seized the opportunity, and Dad stepped in. The two 'hit it off', as they say, and soon my mother married this man and moved into his lonely cobwebbed mansion, hanging her paintings and commandeering the top floor for her studio. She built a patio out the back, a bar in the basement with a dance floor, and installed a piano and zebra-skin couches so they could 'properly receive.' The house would also feature a guest room with a canopy bed and a study, and eventually a tiny room for one child who came very late for two people who'd never thought they'd be married, let alone parents.

These were the people coming over in five minutes, I wanted to tell Anaïs. People who 'dated' and who were introduced to each other through friends on New Year's Eves, people who 'properly received' and didn't sleep around and then brunch with their parents afterwards.

'So could you maybe like leave now?' I nervously fiddled with the phone. 'And, I don't know, come back once they're here? I'll call a car service?'

Anaïs realised I wasn't kidding. And, like that, her look became one of disgust; the kind someone might flash when they notice the person across from them has long, curled fingernails. 'No, I khant jest leave and like calm bach,' she snapped, doing the best imitation a Frenchwoman could do of a California Valley girl.

None of her anger was directed at my parents, of course. Anaïs was upset at this child in front of her, masquerading as an adult. 'What's going to happen is *zis*,' she explained. 'We're going to make some coffee, and I'm going to take a shower, so we're ready when they're here.'

Within minutes the door rang. And, over coffee, I tried to prep Mom and Dad for what I thought would be the big revelation – that there was a woman in my bedroom.

'Did I mention I'm seeing Anaïs?'

'Yes, you did,' my mother said, 'and she sounds grand.'

'Well, she's sure excited to see you.' I bit my lip. 'Oh. Here she is. Ha. Ha. Hi, Anaïs.'

Anaïs came out of my bedroom and introduced herself. Everyone, to my shock, behaved like real adults, and soon we were at brunch. Granted Mom and Dad still called me Johnny in front of her, and asked Anaïs if she was a Democrat like me, but something seemed different, I could tell. It was if they were thanking Anaïs or doing what they couldn't – that is, make me a man.

Soon Anaïs would return to Paris, where employment for a French actress is a bit easier to find. But before we could embark on a drawn-out, likely-to-die, long-distance relationship, two towers would fall on Manhattan, anthrax would show up in the US mail, war would be declared, and that reptile-brained instinct humans have to procreate during times of crisis would push me onto an Air France flight to accompany Anaïs to a wedding in France. There, I'd find out first-hand that terror sex does have consequences, and three months later we were pregnant on the Pont-Neuf deciding whether to marry.

When I broke the big news to Mom and Dad, I separated it into two chunks, thinking it would be easier for them to swallow. The 'Anaïs and I are getting married!' generated yays and cheers, so I used the crowd noise to sneak in my follow-up 'and Anaïs is pregnant'. They rolled with it. Plus an engagement meant they could throw a party in Georgetown and let all the guests figure out the math of who and what came first. What they didn't appreciate was when I called back a week later in a panic, explaining in an existential crisis kind of way that I'd had second thoughts and that maybe it all was a big mistake. I'd forgotten, of course, that women like my mother didn't make big mistakes. Nor did they offer up advice for something as large as this. It was crude. And I was supposed to be smart enough to know what to do by now and how to react and, especially, how to decipher what she was trying to say without her having to spell it out for me.

'What aren't you sure about, dear?' she asked. There was silence on the end for once. The blaring TV in the living room had been turned off.

'About having a child and all this with Anaïs. Maybe we shouldn't get married. Maybe we should just – I don't know. Anaïs'll be fine.' I made it sound as if I was letting Anaïs travel to Mexico with friends for a week without me.

There was silence on the phone.

'No, you're right. Anaïs and the child will be fine without you.' Mom's voice had hardened, giving her the air of a pissed-off Elizabeth Taylor. 'You're the one I'm worried about, because I will cut you off, boy.'

She said *boy* like a Texan and that was the end of our talk. The anger in her voice was an ominous warning of where my life would head if I remained a child. I would marry this girl and get on with this life that my clumsy ass had luckily stumbled over. 'Besides,' she concluded, 'I sent out the invites for the engagement party.'

My mother didn't understand why I was coming clean to her anyway. It was Anaïs I needed to talk to. And so it was there on that Parisian night, with Anaïs *bah*-ing me on the Pont-Neuf, that everything suddenly fell into place.

I should probably explain at this point something of Anaïs's family, who, some critics might suggest, were getting the riskier deal, embracing an unemployed American writer.

As luck would have it, they were not a conventional crew. Anaïs's father, Hughes, resembles Led Zeppelin's Robert Plant, and in France has almost the same notoriety. He led a rock group in the 1970s called Malicorne, which could best be described as a French Jethro Tull; a band whose Druid influences mixed bagpipes with heavy guitar and gave the group a cultlike following it still enjoys today. Anytime Anaïs works on a play or film, there's invariably a roadie/gaffer/lighting grip who stands slack-jawed when he finds out who her dad is, asking if he can have a signed copy of something, anything. Malicorne is the group sound engineers who buy good weed listen to.

My father-in-law lived the cliché you'd expect from a successful ex-rock star. He had an insane apartment in Montmartre that overlooked Paris. He was on wife number four, a wife younger than his daughter (my future wife), a point he'd bring up to me every so often in the future. He'd also recently become a father again. But, aside from his Benjamin Button life cycle, Hughes was hardly the overbearing *beau-père* so many of my friends who'd recently married were lamenting. When they'd complain about their fathers-in-law, citing the age-old tropes of pressure to earn more money or the feeling of not measuring up, I could only sit back and smile at what fortune had bestowed upon me.

Hughes had known the fallow periods of being an artist. He'd written jingles for ads and had gone out of pocket to produce albums his labels didn't want. He'd also spent his fair share of time on the beach, so my (un)employed status didn't really faze him. Was he going to be the dad who shows up on Christmas Eve with a reindeer sweater to take the kids to the Galeries Lafayette shop window decorations? Of course not. But he would jump into a Kuala Lumpur pool fully clothed with you on New Year's Eve, or treat you to a four-hour Montmartre lunch, then walk you around Paris to see his old haunts, all the time insisting we let our wives' calls go to voicemail.

During these post-*déjeuner* strolls, Hughes filled me in on the family's backstory: how Anaïs was technically a countess and how she (well, they) came from an illustrious French aristocrat family, the kind whose name has two *des* and one *la* in it, the kind whose tradition of having at least one male relative in the military each generation dates all the way back to the Fifth Crusade.

This proud military lineage, which included General Leclerc, who liberated Paris with De Gaulle, was broken (of course) by Hughes, who became the first male not to fall in line, choosing instead, as he told me, 'the second-best option: French folk rock star.' And, in keeping with this, Anaïs grew up very differently from how I might have imagined a French aristocrat would. Her childhood wasn't one of running around the château in a Burberry dress chased by a British nanny, but following her dad's group on tour, sleeping with her sister on leather restaurant banquettes during post-concert band dinners.

Like Hughes, none of Anaïs's aunts or uncles or cousins would fill out the portraits of what I expected the noble French to be, either. They were more like the Kennedys, actually, meaning everyone voted Left, each liked to drink, and there were a few tragic deaths here and there. Like poor British uncle Tony, who, after arriving from London at Gare du Nord, was run over after he stepped off the sidewalk, because, as a Brit, he was looking the wrong way.

They also had a tendency to shun their titles, thanks in large part to Hughes's generation – counterculture sixties kids known in France as the *soixante-huitards* ('68ers – in reference to the protest of 1968) – who'd run from, rather than embraced, the wave of patronage that had broken upon them. Hughes had forgone inheriting the château (which comes with being first in line), seeing that the deal required him to live in it full time, something his music business wouldn't allow. Anaïs's aunt had become the first female bus driver in France. Other aunts were musicians, some were professors, and one uncle was a journalist. The most aristocratic thing about them was that everyone spoke at least three languages. They'd all grown up in Spain. And all, except for one, had married foreigners.

Our wedding, we decided, should be held in Paris. That way, Anaïs wouldn't have to fly, and we could plan something I wasn't really comfortable with in a language I wasn't really comfortable speaking. So the invites were sent out, the reception booked, and before long we were saying our vows at the American Church in Paris on a nippy spring day in late April. The fact that the American Church was Protestant (a rarity in Paris), with a reverend from Richmond, gave it allure. I was a sucker for Pastor Rogers's Virginia drawl. Yes, he called me Don (which I corrected each time) and called Anaïs Ah-Nye-is (which she let ride). But, for us, Pastor Rogers could do no wrong.

Just as I was attracted to the cold rationalism of Cartesian France, Anaïs was equally giddy to marry into American PowerPointed pragmatism, which is exactly what Rogers offered when he met with us to discuss the wedding and the pitfalls of modern marriage. Inside his office, in the bowels of the church, Rogers refrained from talking about faith or Jesus or the church's stance on abortion, and instead jumped quickly into discussing the three traps that await the modern couple. We weren't to worry, though, as each, he felt, had its solution. For the in-law issues? Spend Thanksgiving with one family, Christmas with another. For money issues? Have individual bank accounts and one common account. And for sex? Take long weekends without the kids. The fact that she was hearing this from a man of the cloth was downright exotic for Anaïs – and nothing like the abstractions of the Catholic priests or nuns whom she'd feared at school.

Rogers even had a response to Anaïs's having been married before. 'Well, I'm not going to say it didn't happen,' he started. 'Look,' he then leaned forward and spoke in a hushed tone as if he were a coach drawing up a play, 'I like to look at life a lot like a lawn, and that part over there that's a little muddy? Well, we're just going to cover it with a white sheet and walk on it.' I really didn't get this metaphor. If a white sheet were walked over, wouldn't mud seep through? And isn't covering up the past with a sheet kind of, I don't know, repressed? But Anaïs was sold and beaming at him, and soon we were shaking hands and out the door. We were married the next week.

For any marriage to be official in France, however, the grand tradition of *laïcité* (the French concept of secularism) requires each couple to first pass before *la mairie* (town hall), regardless of one's religion or gender. There you stand before the mayor of your arrondissement (in our case the Tenth), wearing a tricoloured sash, and swear an oath of civic union, while the portrait of the French president (in our case, Jacques Chirac) beams down on you both.

Since the mayor (you hope) has other stuff to do during the week, weddings are held on select days, and since there's no way around a town hall marriage, there's a cattle-call-type crowd in the lobby of each *mairie* on Saturday mornings. If you're getting married in the diverse Tenth, you'll wait your turn with Indian, African, Orthodox Jewish and Arabic brides, all decked out in traditional wear, milling around with cellphones and taking turns smiling in group photos on the red carpeted steps leading up to the main hall.

It's what city planners dreamed of when they imagined integration, and yet it's all still very bureaucratically French. IDs are passed around. You sign a lot of stuff you don't understand and, at the end, you receive a *livret de famille* (family notebook), a family passport which you'll be called upon to present at the most solemn and dire life events. There's a page for births (and deaths) of children, births and deaths of parents, naming of children and divorce judgments – the only information people will remember you by two hundred years from now. Crucially, there's only one *livret* per family (and there are no copies), so in our family there's an obligatory biannual panic to find it, with Anaïs hysterically screaming, *'Le livret de famille est perdu!!'*

Following our swearing--in ceremony, an entourage made up mostly of French (the Americans were too jet lagged to make the 10am call time) migrated to a café across the street. There was Yolaine, Anaïs's aunt who had become France's first female bus driver, and who's now a deputy in French Parliament for the Macron party. There was Hughes, of course, joined by his two little children (Anaïs's brother and sister), who were serving as the flower girl and page boy. And there was Laure, Anaïs's mother, strolling next to Hughes, looking like she had thirty years earlier, when she'd married Hughes at eighteen, having met him when Hughes's band played at her debutante party.

All of us commandeered part of the café, and soon Champagne was brought out and everyone drank a little too fast considering it was still only 11am. Cops and deliverymen, barflies, card players and pensioners raised their cups of coffee and glasses of Chablis to the jeunes mariés in the back. Anaïs sat on my knee, and all I wanted to do was stop time in that little hole in the wall and let the rest of the marriage finish itself.

Unfortunately, that wasn't possible. Our formal wedding was across town in the posh Seventh Arrondissement on the Quai d'Orsay, the thoroughfare that runs along the Seine's Left Bank in the shadow of the Eiffel Tower. It was a fifteen-minute metro ride that by car felt as if it took two hours.

There Pastor Rogers called me John for the first time, and I was so thrilled I kissed Anaïs to celebrate. We left the church to music that Hughes had composed for the event, and from the steps Anaïs tossed a giant bouquet into the frisky April air toward a pile of French and American single women each trying to be so polite to the others that nobody bothered to reach up to catch it. The bouquet hit the ground with a thud, followed by a group-wide sigh of pity. We were hitched.

We topped off the ceremony aboard a *péniche* drifting up and down the Seine long into the next morning, the boat brimming with Parisians and New Yorkers all of whom were enjoying something they'd never seen or done before.

Apart from Notre Dame and the Louvre, the Parisians weren't very helpful in identifying many of the illuminated landmarks we were drifting by, which led to awkward mis-understandings.

'What's that? French Parliament?' the American would ask.

'I don't know. What do you think?' the French person would say.

'Are you being sarcastic?' the American would then reply.

The highlight of the night was watching my parents seated next to Anaïs's grandparents, as they were the same age and had much in common. Since my mother had lived in Paris in the 1950s, she knew Paris quite well, and she and Anaïs's grandmother compared neighbourhoods, nightclubs and styles, trading lines in French and English. Their husbands (both veterans of World War II) concentrated more on Paris in the 1940s: the liberation of Paris and D-Day, the merriment of the night prompting my father to quip, 'Yeah, but Alain, six weeks and you guys fold? I mean, jeez!'

When I first met Anaïs in New York in 2000, I of course didn't know she was a French blue blood. And, even if I had, I probably wouldn't have cared that much. Nobility doesn't mean squat in New York. Sure, you gloss over a couple of aristocrat names here and there in the *Vanity Fair* event pages – Count von Hollenlohe-something-or-other at the Hamptons Film Festival, and you wonder who that person is, only because they're standing next to real American royalty like Ryan Gosling or The Rock.

And the French aren't too impressed themselves, either. Half of those claiming some sort of royal status probably aren't even aristocrats, Anaïs would later tell me. They're 'usurpers', meaning they'd usurped the title from someone and made it their own. And there were a bunch of usurpers apparently in the States, she said, where people were less equipped to sniff out these fakes.

I was intrigued by this usurping business, not just because it's such a great verb, but because there was also a Barry Lyndon-like treachery my life needed more of. Anaïs told me that in France usurping happens all the time. Some bourgeois *arriviste* (social climber) would assume an aristocratic name as a way to gain an invitation to a Sotheby's auction or a lower bank rate, or, in the case of 1970s politician Valéry Giscard (he later became Valéry Giscard d'Estaing), the position of French president.

There was actually a story about Anaïs's own family name being usurped. Some cad had gone so far as to write to Anaïs's great-grandfather asking permission to use the name. He was thanked for his polite request, of course, but no, that was completely impossible. And soon a social equivalent of a cease-and-desist letter was sent out. The usurper ran with the name anyway.

This would start what Anaïs's family would call the 'fake branch'. Although there was outrage at the outset, eventually the fake branch would prove to be a convenient alibi. If there was ever a wayward cousin the family was embarrassed by, all anyone needed to say was 'Oh, he's from the fake branch.'

That gross far-right politician who's always yapping on TV? Never met him, certainly a usurper.

As our boat cut through the waves of the Seine, I had the idea that some of the wedding guests might have thought I was a usurper. I mean, the parallels were obvious. I meet my target in a New York bar. Claim a sketchy profession. I have a *von* at the beginning of my name. Perhaps those 'Well, John's done quite well for himself, hasn't he', nudge-nudge wink-wink comments I'd noticed were meant to convey I was part of some club, and that, by marrying Anaïs, my ship had come in. But it hadn't, and probably wouldn't. And who cared? If anything, our story was even better. I'd fallen for a French countess thinking she was a French waitress, which in itself sounded even more Hollywoodian (and thus authentically American aristocratic).

Just then our boat passed underneath the Pont-Neuf, its Parisian beige stone radiating over the water. And when we came out on the other end, a sort of premonition seized me. All that I was about to embark on could have easily slipped by the wayside had I not kissed Anaïs that fateful night. None of the intricate French dinners I'd eventually learn to master, nor the weird vacations I'd eventually grow to fear. None of the odd jobs I'd land, nor the strange situations my bumbling French would put me in. Perhaps not even the ratty French-American kids we'd eventually have together. None of these glorious things would have come to pass had the dancing pregnant woman at the stern of the boat not assured me, in all her French frankness, that *bah*, we could always just get divorced.

CHAPTER TWO

TWO MORE WEDDINGS
AND A PIG

LITTLE DID I KNOW THAT OUR WEDDING would be talked about for years to come. Not because it was especially memorable or elaborate, but because, peculiarly, it had been held *in Paris* – ten metro stops away from our home. This, to my new French friends, was a peculiar and perhaps typically American thing to do. Had I been French, it would have taken place deep in the foothills of rural France, where young Parisian couples return to a drafty old church and then a tent in a field in a hard-to-find hometown, to plant the seeds of their future togetherness in the *terre* whence they came. While I, in the crowd, dutifully applaud and wish them the best, wondering why we couldn't have done this in Paris.

French weddings start with an index-card-sized RSVP and a return envelope, whereas American invitations always need to go that extra buck-wild yard. I've received American 'Save the date – heads up!' cards a *year and a half* in advance, which were then followed by eCards with passwords linking me to websites that asked me the song I wanted to dance to, along with my dinner seating preference, almost as if the wedding were an airline seating reservation. There would be vouchers for golf, and registry lists that were so precise there was no room left for improvisation or personal touch. It was either the sleeping bag or the Coleman cooking stove for the trip to the Andes. With such tact, I almost expected a third option of paying down the Amex card for that trip to the Himalayas. (I've heard this is actually done.)

But you get what you pay for in the States. I've been to American weddings on private islands where the kids wear life vests the whole night. Others had photo booths and twenty-member big bands and fireworks. One even had an upstairs cocaine room.

The French gift demands are usually more modest. They'll ask you to chip in for a trip they want to take eventually or the Charles Eames chair they've been eyeballing for the living room. And that's it. Fifty euros or less, which is great when you're a guest, not so great when it's your wedding. For ours, we forgot to specify what we wanted people to contribute to, so they assumed we didn't want anything at all.

But, with French invites, I always scratch my head about where they are going to take place. There is often nothing to go on. Villeneuve-lès-Avignon? Vitry-le-François? Saint-Remy-en-Bouzemont-Saint-Genest-et-Isson? Where the fuck were these places? Not in Paris, that's for sure. In fact, the more hyphens a place in France has, the less likely you're able to find it on a map.

I'd conveniently forgotten, of course, these were the towns my friends had told me they'd come from when I'd asked naïvely if they were from Paris. 'Bien sûr que non, John,' they'd reply, then rattle off some convoluted name while I sipped my drink, having no idea where that was, but already fully convinced it sucked. You know a place is forgettable when the person describing it says what it's close to, and you don't even know *that* place. 'It's close to Vierzon, John. It's close to Mulhouse. You know Béthune? It's right near there.' Got it.

Honoré de Balzac was right. In the end, Paris is a city full of people from the provinces, most of whom, if they had their way and didn't need a job, would move back to the small town or village they came from. Unfortunately, in France, there's no other city that offers as many good-paying jobs, so Paris it is. Americans may think of it as 'the city of light', but, for a lot of Parisians, Paris is an upscale jail, one that allows you to leave on occasional weekends to marry your concubine.

There's also the economic side. No French person wants to spend a lot of money renting a large wedding venue in Paris when you can easily blag a giant manor from an uncle, or call up a cousin who has a farmhouse with a big field. And, if that's the case, the invitation will feature the key words *soirée champêtre*, which is a fancy way to say bucolic or rural, but which I've learned really means 'tent out back.'

And, I must admit, the *idea* of a *champêtre* is romantic. When I first was invited to one, I imagined lanterns and candles hidden in acres of high grass, women and girls with wildflowers in their hair, men with daisies on their lapels, dogs running freely, and forest elves passing out hors d'oeuvres. As the years have gone by, I've grown more accustomed to my friends' pitches. I wait like clockwork for the moment they'll promote the facility of on-site child care, how they'll have a crew of babysitters around the clock and how we'll be able to dance into the morning without worrying about noise. 'And, you know what,

John?' they'll finish. 'We're even going to cook a pig in the ground!'

The pig-cooking couple in question had been dear friends for ages. They lived near us in Paris and had been at our wedding, so not attending theirs was simply *hors de question*. They, too, were a couple who'd gotten the order of operations mixed up. Their children were our children's age. We'd attended baptisms, housewarming parties, and now, ten years later, we were going back in time to attend their wedding.

With any *champêtre* wedding, accommodations are going to be limited. And, since we weren't part of the happy few who'd reserved the three rooms at the inn two kilometres from the reception a year in advance, we found ourselves staying at a wild-card B&B a windy thirty-minute drive away. This happens often to unorganised people like us, and since we don't want to stay at these second-choice, dingy bed and breakfasts too long (meaning more than one night), we usually leave Paris by car Saturday morning with the goal of being at the church service in the afternoon. Sure, we risk arriving late or missing the service altogether, but I'm okay with that.

Usually French ceremonies are not 'kiss the bride and we're out' affairs. They're an entire Catholic service with a wedding tacked on at the end. The churches are pretty strict about what they allow during a service, too, meaning it's rare to find a Joan Baez acoustic guitar solo sung by an old friend from university, and even rarer to find a church that's actually warm.

French churches were not built for comfort. There are no wheelchair ramps, or well-identified fire exits, or carpeted aisles. If anything, country churches are allegories of tasteful decay. On an altar, there leans a painting that may be a Giotto original, and yet next to it sits a pigeon nest, and that paint that's chipping on the ceiling above you is actually from a relief dating back to the Papal Schism.

What's impressive about these places is that you feel the appreciation of time passed, but not the weight of history. You forget the countless services held for those claimed by unending plagues and wars, along with all those silent prayers whispered by those who suffered from God knows what during the Middle Ages or World War I. All that's left is the quiet light of the stained-glass windows, the smoothed-over alabaster entryways, and the arctic chill that rains down whenever I sit in those hardwood pews. There are other Parisian attendees in a similar bind, and I can spot them easily. The men have those typical scruffy Zach Galifianakis, Right Bank Parisian beards and are usually looking at their phones, gyrating their legs as a way to keep their white Conversed feet warm. At least that was the look of the man sitting in the pew in front of me, the one who'd curiously leaned a trumpet on the wall next to him, which would foreshadow his whipping it out following the service, leading a cortège of sorts through the village to the reception, tooting us the whole way there.

This wasn't my first cortège. Hughes had shepherded one up the slopes of Montmartre, beginning at the *mairie* of the Eighteenth Arrondissement, when Anaïs's sister was married, that ended at his apartment atop Sacré-Coeur, beating a drum while others trumpeted and clarinetted next to him. The tourists who'd come to visit Sacré-Coeur that day took photos. Some even threw money.

In this pig-cooking case, the locals of the village were less enthralled by our Parisian Chuck Mangione. He wasn't from the famed group Malicorne. That was certain. He also played alone and hadn't practised much, so the toots grew tired by the time we reached the boulangerie. Soon he was holding up traffic to get wind, and by the time a local mentioned he should get a job we'd abandoned him en masse, ducking into cars that would take us the remaining five hundred yards to the cocktails that awaited us.

Any French meal, large or small, features what's called an *apéro* – short for *aperitif*, which usually involves drinks and olives or *saucisson sec* or chips of some sort served in small portions in an informal setting. *Apéros* are a way to meet your fellow dinner guests while sipping on something bubbly; champagne or a kir or a beer before you get down to the business of eating.

Each French wedding has its own *apéro*, which is usually in the form of a giant champagne orgy. Whatever money the marrying couple saves on renting a space in Paris proper, they plunge into the champagne. There are no half-measures with this ritual, since they know their wedding will be judged not on the decor or on the meal or even on the locale, but on the quality of champagne.

Wedding *apéros* are also the combustible moment when you drink the most and eat the least, thanks to a rural setting where the meal usually arrives very late. The problem with *champêtre* is that logistics are not on your side. It's difficult rustling up three hundred meals from a small truck in a muddy field. I've watched rotisseries implode, truck batteries run out of juice or, in our case this time, the pig in the ground not cooking as fast as our hosts thought it would.

My groom friend explained to me that cooking a pig in a dirt pit comes from French Polynesia, and that it's a complex process that can take several days of preparation and time. It involves digging the pit, firing it up, dressing the pig with rubs and oil, and cooking it for approximately nine hours, depending on its size. My concern was that, after the second hour of the *apéro*, we weren't yet on hour nine of the pig process. But, since the sun was out, the news didn't particularly worry the groom. The champagne was flowing, and it was a perfect chance to enjoy the mountain views. Two hours later, though, the sun was gone, and the fun was over. A damp cold had set in, and we found ourselves still clinging to champagne glasses as we ran to the car to warm up while the dinner continued to cook.

At country weddings, the temperature always yo-yos. The church will be cold. The walk from the church will be hot. The reception will be hot, then cold, and the late-night dancing will be frigid. The challenge is to dress accordingly while maintaining a certain look. Women will often bring shawls or sweaters that they somehow hold on to discreetly. But, since men are kind of stuck with a blazer and tie (and there's no way a Patagonia fleece is acceptable), I've started sporting the sweater vest underneath the blazer. It's borderline, but passable, and it's saved me countless times.

When the pig was ready and we'd been seated at our table, Anaïs was no longer hungry, and I was cold drunk. Since things were running late, the wedding speeches kicked off immediately, even while the food was being served, and this was a relief, seeing as there's nothing more appetising for me than watching people bomb onstage.

For reasons I still don't understand, the French have never been able to find that happy alchemy of funny and serious. French toasts are either tear-felt emotional or lampoon tacky, but nothing in between. I've seen a woman read a four-page cheat sheet that lasted an extra twenty minutes because she wept the whole way through. I've also watched five men strip down to jockstraps with rainbow Afro wigs and dance to 'It's Raining Men', urging us to clap along. I've watched skits performed in shark costumes, the actors bent over double, laughing at their inside joke, while the audience stares on, their faces looking as if they had just smelled ammonia.

While the night's speeches wore on, I spotted the best man at the bar. His name was Yves, and he was looking distressed, staring in frustration at the cocktail napkin bearing his speech. Having watched many toast hara-kiris in past years, I'd promised myself that if I ever saw someone in need of a quick punch-up or encouragement, I'd help. I've been told I give a pretty good toast; I've even thought about penning a screenplay à la *Wedding Crashers* about a professional toastmaster, hired by couples to make their famous wedding speech. In the film, the main character would spend a week with the couple to get to know them and learn their stories, which he'd then incorporate into his speech. The twist would come, of course, when the toastmaster falls for the bride, and all hell breaks loose. *But Seriously* was the working title, and currently those are the two words I've written of the script.

Soon, Yves and I were chatting, me advising him that the best speech he could give would be something simple and heartfelt. 'Don't worry about following the napkin,' I told him. 'Napkins always trip you up. *C'est nul, les serviettes!*'

'*T'as raison*' (you're right), he snorted in his glass, '*ça s'improvise,*' at which point I left him to gather his thoughts, convinced I had put him on the right track.

Unfortunately, once onstage, our man did indeed toss the napkin aside, then he unscrewed the microphone from the podium and walked into the crowd like a nightclub act. Before I could take my seat, he'd launched into criticising the father of the groom's speech (which had preceded his) as one 'filled with sappy nostalgia'. 'But are we even surprised by this *merde* from *Monsieur Daddy Nostalgie*, anyway?' he squeaked through the feedback, aping the father of the groom as if he were a dithering fool.

The speech went painfully on. An *enculé* (whose translation is *fuckhead* but which literally means 'done in the ass') was thrown out; an *enfoiré* (whose translation means *shithead* but which literally means 'covered in excrement') soon followed. It was a poetic speech, sure, and for a crowning coup de grâce, as several moved in to seize the microphone, the bard told my friend, the groom, in front of his stunned table, that he'd like a crack at his daughter (who was seventeen). Then he proceeded to dive into the nearby pool, in full tux. Music came on. Everyone applauded mercifully, then quickly turned to their plates, which were now getting cold, letting the best man make his way on his own to the shallow end, where he'd exit the pool and the wedding altogether.

Seeing a toast end up in the water was shocking, not just because it was so audaciously punk, but because it was so cold out. A mild hypothermia had seized me by then, which no buried pig fire in the world could thaw. The cake was cut, and soon the faint drumbeat of music began emanating from another tent, in another part of the cow field.

With it being *champêtre* and all, I scampered through the high grass thinking I'd find a warm whisky, only to catch the groom pitted against an intransigent, locally hired DJ who'd conveniently forgotten to bring a converter, which would have synced the amp to my friend's iTunes. The two were on the verge of blows – the DJ unable to understand why my outraged friend didn't have confidence in his 'trusted CD collection'.

Little did both men realise their collections or *mixes* (pronounced *meeks*), if put side by side, were fairly identical. Each was eighties French pop fused with eighties French disco fused with eighties French crooner. Songs that refuse to go away, songs that everyone says they hate but everyone knows the lyrics to. In a way, watching the two men argue gave me a glimpse into what it must be like for a far right and far left voter watching current French politics. Although they duke it out, the far-left and far-right resemble each other more than they think, and the songs they sing have sounded the same since the Mitterrand era.

At the outset I danced only because I wanted to warm up, but soon the floor was taken over by those doing *le rock*, the 1950s-styled Lindy Hop you see mostly in Frank Capra films, one which involves twirling your partner around as if you were at a Princeton tea dance. Americans invented *le rock*, but not one American under seventy knows how to dance it. I've been in France sixteen years, and I'm still lost. Bill Haley and the Comets comes on, those around me pivot in unison and dance in time, and all I can do is fake-smile and hold Anaïs by the hands while spinning her around in a circle as if it was 'Hava Nagila' at a bar mitzvah.

The one wedding song I'm able to sing from start to finish is Jacques Brel's *'Ne me quitte pas'* ('Don't Leave Me'), and it's only because Brel pronounces each *triste mot* slowly and with perfect clarity. Plus there are only four or five words per line. Any time I hear Brel's simple piano chords begin the song, I pipe up. And, although it's dreary, I treat it like Journey's 'Don't Stop Believing', belting out each *Ne me quitte pas* as if it's my last. It's a sad spectacle. The rest of the time I've been told '*Tu chantes yaourt, John*', which means I sing with 'yogurt in my mouth' – mumbling words, while smiling as if I know the song perfectly, because in my mind I do.

I soon broke from the fun and went outside the tent, where I spotted a younger group in their twenties huddled together, and I could tell by their snickering that they, too, hated the music. They were also high as shit. It's always an odd feeling when you're over forty and you're trying to smoke weed with people half your age, especially when they don't speak your native language. Since you have seniority, they're sort of obliged to make room, but it's rarely done with enthusiasm. You've crashed their moment and suddenly transformed a joint with friends into one of polite obligation. And you know this, but you're puffing with them anyway, because as an older person, you've earned the right to invade people's personal space in the pursuit of getting high.

So I butted in and, before I knew it, I was passed a cigarette the size of an asparagus stem. The hashish high hit like lightning, and soon I was too paranoid to go back into the tent. Oh, and the young people I felt so close to five minutes ago? They'd bailed, leaving me to wander aimlessly in my rumpled suit looking for our car while Scorpion's 'Winds of Change' played in the distance to a raucous crowd.

This wasn't the first time Anaïs and I had experienced French wedding blackouts, the kind that left one spouse frantically looking for the other for the better part of the night, convinced they'd probably drowned. At one country wedding, Anaïs ducked away to put our baby daughter to bed, making me promise to check in on them after thirty minutes to make sure Anaïs hadn't drifted off to sleep. Promises like these are made in the moment and tend to fall by the wayside when you're smoking outside of a tent, which is where I was thirty minutes after Anaïs and Bibi's bedtime departure, this time with Jules, a friend from Paris.

'Oh, I put some cocaine in it.' Jules casually assured me when I laid into my third toke.

'Sorry?' I asked, eyes wide.

'*Oui*, it's just I can't sniff that stuff. My nose won't let me.'

Apparently, the immorality of handing me a hard drug without warning hadn't dawned on my friend. Within moments, it was I who was on the dance floor dancing *le rock*, throwing a woman through my legs and swinging her around my shoulders like an MMA fighter, all to the claps of an impressed crowd. I'd not only forgotten I didn't know *le rock*, I'd forgotten to wake Anaïs, who surfaced toward the end of the party with cloudy eyes and bed hair, bitter at me for not holding up my end of the bargain.

All of this I fondly reflected on as I sat hunched over in our car with the heat blasting, picking pig out of my teeth. Soon Anaïs was tapping on the driver's side window, holding a coffee. It was over, and she was driving us home. There was a dense mist out now, and because the GPS couldn't find our coordinates (probably because I couldn't find hyphens on the keyboard), we spent hours finding our B&B. It was so quiet in the country that night, you could still hear the music miles away pulsing behind us as we rolled through the fog, giving the scene all the trappings of Michael Jackson's '*Thriller*' video.

CHAPTER THREE

BRINGING UP BIBI

MY FRIENDS IN THE STATES never, ever, looked to me for advice before I moved abroad. If anything, I was the canary in their life-lesson coal mine. Knowing me had helped them avoid jumping into frozen lakes naked, or playing Three-card Monte in truck stops, or leaving boarding tickets on the bar while you head to the bathroom. However, after I settled in France, the tables turned. I was now a French father and in their eyes this made me a child-raising guru, one who personifies all those *Bringing Up Bébé* techniques they'd read about but not yet seen in practice. 'Share with us, O wise one,' their eyes would plead.

Like all good Americans, I, too, assumed the vaunted *système* and *méthode française* was like some genius super-computer; all I had to do was plug my kids into it and watch it work. They would grow up to have manners, dress tastefully and harbour the astonishing capacity to sit through an adult dinner while also doing my taxes. As my American friends would be wringing their hands over how many timeouts to give, and riffling through books on how to determine how behind their kid is with those early milestones, I'd be in

France, where the only thing they make better than wine is children. In a way, I felt like the idiot son who'd inherited his father's Forbes 500 company, the one whose sole job was just to not drive it into the ground.

In reality, my role has turned out a little differently. Let's say somewhere between that of local superfan (the one who roots and cheers and attends each game while the professionals on the field do the work) and that of a World War I grunt (the one who thought it would be a cakewalk but found himself in a long campaign, bogged down in the trenches of teacher strikes, typing on his laptop during horseback-riding class, hunched over homework he can't help his kids with, or lost in some incomprehensible parent–teacher meeting).

My recollection of the early years, as for any parent who didn't sleep, is muddled. By the time we arrived in France, Anaïs was already *très* pregnant. And during the final trimester, while we looked for an apartment and applied for my French residency, consulted with doctors and rushed to hospital checkups, I found little time to research what to expect. The only books I remember buying myself were name books, and whenever Anaïs asked me if I thought that a burping technique had been debunked since Dr Spock or whether we should sing to the baby while it was still in the womb, my replies were one-worded: 'Ella? Sinead? Alistair! I haven't heard that one in a while!' The name, for me, was more important than any holistic environment we could ever provide. A good name could ward off mumps. Also, the naming part was an activity and contribution I understood.

During the doctor's consultations, I found myself checked out half the time, and that was probably for the better. I'm sure I would have freaked if I had grasped the risks of an *amniocentèse* or the 'what-if' scenarios for a potential caesarean. Instead I smiled and waved through all the garbled French, entranced by the ultrasound printouts. 'Anaïs, that's the skull of a Lars, don't you think?' My choice to fly on autopilot was also a defence mechanism to counter being overwhelmed. Adapting to a foreign country had already flooded my hard drive. If you'd met me at the time, you wouldn't have seen a stressed-out person but someone looking as though he'd just been tasered.

Normally when you're feeling useless, as I was, you can find a way to chip in somehow. But since I didn't have a car, or a French driver's licence, and shopping for a stroller or one of those baby bathtubs seemed too daunting, I plunged into tasks such as asking my mother to ship over the chestnut crib I slept in as a baby. Suddenly I found the resolve to discuss with an *ébéniste* (cabinetmaker) how I wanted the crib sanded and what tint it should be lacquered. And when Anaïs waddled into the apartment days before we left for the hospital, asking if I'd packed that overnight suitcase, I, of course, said no, and showed her instead a wooden crib straight out of a Dickens novel. There were no blankets, nor a mattress. 'But,' I said, 'won't it be awesome to take a picture of the baby in this and compare it with my photo when I was a kid?' I was still thinking a lot about myself.

Anaïs insisted her doctor be her long-time ob-gyn, Marie-José, whose clinic was located in the western suburb of Le Chesnay, one of those Paris 1970s planned developments cut out of a Jacques Tati film, a place where everything looks a bit too organised and manicured to be human. The plant beds are there. The cul-de-sacs wind here. And that lawn in front of the office building has never been walked on, ever. While we waited for our appointments, I'd find myself strolling around Le Chesnay looking for a café, feeling like a clay figurine in an architect's model. This wasn't at all where I expected to become a French father. I'd pictured, I don't know, hospital steps from the Seine where nurses in white headscarves would lead me down hushed mahogany-trimmed halls past smoking doctors to see my beautiful newborn. Instead, Bibi's official place of birth would be more like a French Scottsdale, Arizona.

Whatever problems I had with Le Chesnay, however, were shelved when I met Marie-José, who looked like an older Brigitte Bardot. She sported tasteful gold jewellery and a solid tan, and although she was on-call *en permanence*, she never deigned to wear Crocs, and her blonde shock of hair was impeccable. She carried index cards, one for each patient, which she kept nestled in the front pocket of her scrubs. It was as if they were cue cards and she was an actress shooting the role of a doctor. Marie-José also happened to be very sympathetic to my plight. She'd speak slowly to both of us, sometimes even in English, and she always called Anaïs 'ma biche' ('my dear', but *deer* in the animal sense). I found this adorable. It was as if Marie-José were making a play on words in English for my sake.

Bibi was born on a beautiful late June afternoon. I can remember the weather because I was taking banal pictures of trees and flowers in the clinic's garden five minutes before her arrival. Sure, I probably should have been at Anaïs's side, but I felt it important to document the last vestiges of life as I knew it. By the time I wandered into the operating room, Anaïs was mid-labour and, before I could put my mask on, Marie-José had handed me a pair of scissors to cut Bibi's ropelike umbilical cord.

I was a part of the process now. Waiting on the sidelines was over. Minutes later I was whisked into a room filled with *couveuses* – glass pod incubators with babies inside. When I scanned the room, I saw five or six swaddled newborns and one miniature 1920s actress. Bibi had round eyes the size of saucers, chalky white skin and dainty fingers that seemed already capable of needlepoint. There wasn't an ounce of baby fat on her, not a touch of red or rash.

'*Elle est si fine* [she's so delicate], so girly,' friends who dropped by would say, 'she looks just like John!' I'd become an official patriarch, the so-called summit of a man's virile and masculine life, only to be told that I resembled Lillian Gish. My role would soon expand, however, as it came time to register Bibi's name at the *mairie* (town hall). French law demands this be done no later than three days after the birth, and usually the chore falls on the father, who's not convalescing.

Again, I strolled down that soulless cul-de-sac past the single Le Chesnay mailbox, to where a woman at the *mairie* asked me to fill out forms and print the name *Bibi* clearly, and handed me ten copies of Bibi's birth certificate and a welcome packet, as if Bibi had just booked a cruise.

It was silly, but at the same time this pomp and circumstance and traditional fluff meant something. Just like how the mayor of the Tenth wore his sash when he oversaw our civil marriage, there was an old-school formality to registering my child's name that I appreciated. It made a father feel needed. I could be helpful! Look. I'm signing stuff.

Since my only responsibility was the name, I felt doubly guilty months after her birth when not one person had said the following: 'Bibi. That's a nice name.' Instead we heard 'Yeah, but what's her real name?' or '*Bay bay*, you mean?' As if I'd pronounced my own child's name wrong.

When they'd ask, and invariably they did, we'd give them the long blurb that *Bibi* was a Scandinavian name, that Anaïs had always loved the Swedish actress Bibi Andersson, who played the bubbly counter to dreary Liv Ullmann in all those Bergman movies ('Whose movies?' being their usual response). Plus *Bibi* meant 'sparkler of life', we told them, which made sense considering how her hazel eyes flashed like high beams the first time I saw her in the *maternité*. Hazel, of course, would be her middle name.

But the main reason we loved the name *Bibi* was that you could pronounce it the same way in both English and French. It would facilitate things, we thought. And yet many Americans would insist on saying her name as *bébé*, like the French word for baby. These people saw Bibi's name as a way to go the extra mile with French when it wasn't necessary, just to show you how Francophile they really were. These people sucked, surely, but they weren't as bad as the subset of French who'd always cite the name of a popular French animation series called *Bibi Phuck* (Bibi the Seal), which in French is pronounced *Bibi Fuck*. *Merci*.

After a week or so, the three of us were in residence at our apartment, and within hours I was learning words on the fly I'd never used before, some of which were in English, such as *le nesting* and *le baby phone*. To make things more complicated, some terms were in English but were not used the same way. For example, a *body* (pronounced *buddy*) is a onesy and the word *biberon* doesn't mean a bib but a baby bottle. I learned this, of course, the hard way, when Anaïs, bedridden, asked me to hand her Bibi's *biberon*, and I tossed her a bib.

'I said *biberon*! Are you trying to be funny?'

'I just gave it to you!'

Anaïs then let forth a series of English words she had learned recently – among them, *airhead* (which she pronounced *air raid*) and *dumbshit* (*dahm-sheet*). For a split second I started looking for this specific dahm-sheet, before realising it was me.

We needed help.

The dream of every young French parent is to score a place in the crèche – the local day-care centre that takes your baby at two-and-a-half months and returns it to you as a perfectly trained three-year-old. This is such a wonderful offer that it's not uncommon for women three months pregnant to throw their name into the hat for a spot. When you tell people you've landed a space in a crèche, they look at you as if you just won the lottery.

Unfortunately for us, Bibi was born during a Parisian baby boom, so the crèche was full. I slumped a bit at the news but Anaïs remained positive. It didn't mean we were screwed. In France, you still have other options, one being an *assistant-maternelle,* a child-care professional who watches your child, along with a few others, *chez elle.*

Bibi's *assistant-maternelle* was Khadija, a French-Moroccan woman who lived near to us, in Barbès. Each morning I'd drop off Bibi, where she'd spend the day with Khadija's three-year-old son, Oman, and another couple's baby, eating and sleeping and riding in a stroller to the park, while Khadija chatted with other *assistantes maternelles*. If Bibi was still asleep when I picked her up, Khadija and I would share a mint tea with her older daughter, Imen, on a large Moroccan couch, the kind that lines the entire wall of the apartment as if it were about to host a wedding reception.

I admit I hadn't envisioned my initial experience of child care going this way, making the trek each day to public housing in the middle of the most densely populated Arabic neighbourhood in Europe to drop off my three-month-old. And yet, as the days passed, I enjoyed passing all the tunics and bearded men in cafés playing dominoes. Soon I was a regular with the local butcher, who knew I liked his halal lamb chops, and the sidewalk vendor next to him, who'd sell me a handful of freshly cut mint for ten centimes, which I'd then toss into Bibi's stroller to make it smell better. Both of them loved the name *Bibi*. They told me it was an old-school Arabic name as well, one usually associated with women born in the 1920s and 1930s, which made me laugh only because it was funny to think of Bibi as the Arabic equivalent of Gertrude.

Of course, any time a system works, you just have to change it, which we did unfortunately, when we succumbed to the subtle peer pressure of our neighbours with kids and opted for a set-up called *garde partagée*. This means sharing a nanny with one or two other families, and using each family's apartment on a rotating basis to host the children. Since there were others with small children in our building, a *garde partagée*, on paper, seemed smart. It would cut down on the long hikes to Barbès (though I secretly loved these), and would allow us to see more of Bibi.

But *garde partagée* is designed for parents with a fixed schedule and work outside of the home, which was the opposite of our situation. On weeks that it was our turn to host, our apartment would be trashed, as it was transformed into a day-care centre for five kids. If there was a train strike and the nanny couldn't come, and since nobody else could leave work, we were expected to step up. *Garde partagée* also gave me an upfront view of what salaried people really think of freelancers – that you're either rich or unemployed, and you definitely have lots of free time. Not a week passed without a call coming from another parent beginning, 'John, I'm stuck at a meeting. Do you mind taking Rio for an extra hour?'

And it wasn't just the different schedules. Everything was up for debate with these people: what park the nanny should take them to, menus, the quality of the carrots. Snack allowance and metro fares were negotiated down to the last centime. *Garde partagée* is one of those instances where you become way too involved in the lives of your neighbours, and it not only ruins your friendship with them, it makes you want to move.

In both cases (*assistant-maternelle* and *garde partagée*) you're paying a *nounou* a salary. Yes, you're helped at the end of the year on your taxes, but it's not free. However, both manners of child care are indicative of a French way of doing things: finding similar people in the same boat, pooling your resources, and painfully working through differences in order to avoid what every Parisian parent dreads the most – being a stay-at-home mom or dad.

The French system is kind of a feminist one. According to a 2018 European Commission report on gender equality, the employment rate of women in France is above 65 per cent (higher than most EU countries), and, surprisingly, 95 per cent of children of those French working mothers (birth through school age) are in child care. (For Americans it's more like 30 per cent.) Not only is the French woman the most active working woman in Europe (well, after Finland), France's fertility rate is one of the highest in the EU (2.1 children per woman). All of this I found bizarrely progressive for a country where a married woman did not have the right to work or have her own bank account until 1965.

Luckily, at the end of that *garde partagée* year, we received word that Bibi had been granted a space in the crèche. Before this, I'd never really bought into the crèche myth. Sure it was great, I told myself, but how great could anything be that's free? This was the American in me talking, the one who'd never dare go to Times Square on New Year's Eve or who finds those Whole Foods taste stands with the giveaway Havarti cheese suspicious.

I found myself eating my words my first day at the crèche, when I entered a wonderful oasis of carpets and stuffed animals, mini-sinks and music, all topped off by Bibi's name written in chalk over a small hook and pigeonhole.

On a normal day, I'd lay Bibi on the padded carpet, roll around with her for five minutes, then watch as she crawled toward fifty-year-olds Jocelyne and Muriel and a team of understudies dressed in black-and-white-striped blouses, which made them look like human border collies. The scene was so enchanting, I'd stay on the carpet long after the other parents had left. Outside seemed rough and horrible. Why not chill in the crèche all day? The thing is, the crèche (like French school, later) doesn't want parents around. You get in the way and your shoes are dirty, and soon Muriel was waking me from my reverie with a 'Monsieur [pointing at her watch], c'est l'heure. Don't you have somewhere to go?'

Like the crèche, Bibi's maternelle (nursery) and élémentaire (primary) school were in our neighbourhood and on the same block. There, I'd again drop Bibi off in the morning (as I would my son Otto, who turned up later), and another border collie would take Bibi in her arms and shoo me away. But whereas the crèche was fairly lenient with arrival times, the maternelle quickly reminds you that the only way for this system to work on such a large scale is for everyone to be on time. Drop-off begins at 8.20am and ends at 8.30, at which point the doors close and there will be no excuses. I've seen parents yelling, 'But I have a meeting at nine!' holding their kid in their arms as collateral, with Margaret, la gardienne, staring through them like fogged glass. And the school is right. There is no real excuse for being late. Every child who attends a Paris public maternelle and élémentaire lives within a football field's distance of the establishment. And, for that very reason, we always cut it close. More times than not, I'd find myself running out the door, yoghurt still in one hand, a backpack in the other, carrying Bibi the entire way to make sure we arrived under the 8.30 wire.

All too often, Bibi was required to sit on the bench in the foyer (called by my new school-gate friend, Fred, le banc de la honte – 'the bench of shame'), waiting for her name to be called so she could walk to her class in single file with the other late ones, like a miniature prison road gang.

Once at *élémentaire*, parents are no longer allowed to enter the establishment. The French system is happy if you want to volunteer for outings or school fairs, but they don't want your daily stress. If you want to be briefed, there's a book every child takes home each day called *le carnet de correspondance*, a laminated journal, which updates parents on homework, planned *sorties* (class outings), school fund drives, and the unfortunate *mot* (*word* from the teacher) that your child has been misbehaving. With the *carnet de correspondance*, the school is not asking you to do too much, just read it and, if required, sign.

And I may add, I was good at the signing part. The kids knew this and would always mention they had a *mot* right when my guard was down. While I was on the phone, they'd hand me the *carnet de correspondance* as a corrupt lawyer would to an unwitting client: 'Just sign here, Papa,' they'd whisper. 'Here ... and ... here in the upper right corner. Thanks, Papa. You're the best.' I'd mark my initials, having no idea if I was promising a donation for the end-of-the-year school fair or agreeing to the messages marked in red felt-tip pen: 'Bibi was insolent ... again' or 'Otto continues to disrupt the class with his talking.'

Just to show how low society can stoop, it turns out these *carnets de correspondance* have been used by thieves to rob apartments. The miscreants comb gyms or karate classes or anywhere kids may leave their backpacks unattended. And since apartment keys in that Eastpak backpack's outer pocket match the houses identified by the *carnet de corre-spondance*, the robbers obtain both your address and the keys. Your child brings back not only a *mot*, but a self-drive van ready to empty your apartment.

After learning this, I erased our address on the *carnet*. 'But, Papa, I'm not allowed,' Otto told me, worried.

'Just tell the teacher to send *me* a *mot*, okay?' The case has been closed.

The French school day is a long slog. Once you start *collège* (at age eleven), school can begin as early as 8am and finish as late as 6pm. That may not sound too crazy, but since Otto and Bibi have extracurricular sports after school on certain days, it's not abnormal for them to leave the house around seven and return home as late as 8pm, looking like exhausted tiny waiters just off their shift. On other days, it's possible they'll have a *trou* (hole), a three-hour break in the middle of the day, where it will fall on them to do homework in a local Starbucks before their final class and before they take the metro to sports across town, in both cases alone. If the Americans can be critiqued for their helicopter parenting, the French should have to answer for this *raised by wolves* style. One of the reasons the days are so long, though, is that the French school week is spread over four and a half days, not five. On Wednesdays, school is only in the morning, while the afternoon is reserved for such extracurricular activities as dance, football, capoeira or *le cirque* (circus).

Often, parents negotiate with their employer for what's called a *4/5e*, which enables them to take Wednesday afternoon off. If that's not possible, grandparents are often flown in like the Army Corps of Engineers. On any given Wednesday, Paris is full of grey-haired people schlepping kids around the metro, holding fencing swords and tutus, backpacks and scooters, as their grandchildren make their way from one activity to another. Neither the grandparent nor the child looks happy. I've always found it interesting that in France, where every group has its cause and every profession eventually goes on strike, grandparents never make a peep. And they should, considering how exploited they are. Some clean apartments. Some cook and shop. And none are ever paid! I've told Bibi or Otto that, should they ever have children and try this with me, I will take them to the *prud'hommes* (labour arbitration court) – and that I'll charge them up the wazoo.

Since so much is compacted into a normal French school day, kids, parents and teachers need a two-week break every six weeks. With all this time to fill, parents often sign their children up for *stages* (internships), which sounds funny when someone tells you their seven-year-old is *interning*. If parents are cruel, they'll sign their kid up for a Mandarin *stage* or English *stage*, but in general *stages* are a two-week complement to whatever extracurricular activity the child is already practising during the year. *Stages* also are often chosen (shockingly) because of their proximity to *les grandparents*.

During these 'fake vacations' (as I called them), we'd often pass on the *stage*, in order to take advantage of a Paris without children. And there *is* a difference. Traffic is thinner, you don't have to book tables for lunch, and there are fewer queues in the boulangeries. And we were the only ones with kids! Anaïs, Bibi, Otto and I would hit the Pompidou Centre or find ourselves at the Musée de l'Histoire Naturelle in the Fifth, looking at the stuffed elephants and lions, and sipping on *chocolats chauds*. During these excursions, I caught a glimpse of what it must be like to raise your child in a livable Paris. It was stunning and made me feel like a good parent. How couldn't I be? My children were skipping in their leather shoes near the Jardin des Plantes looking like an ad for Dior. Unfortunately, this Paris would expire at the strike of 6pm on the last Sunday of *fake vacances*, when all of Paris's children would again descend upon the city, led by their white-haired sentries – the latter looking like the army of the dead from *Game of Thrones*.

I trace Bibi's love of animals to those Sunday excursions to the *Grande Galerie de l'Évolution* in the Natural History Museum. As a toddler, she'd go full actors' studio imitating animals, outlasting friends who'd long moved on to puzzles or drawings. It was as if she'd enter a trance: she'd go to the other side of our local pool and imitate a lion growling and stretching out her paws. The lifeguard would look at me, then watch Bibi leaning her head into the pool to drink like a big cat. This trait still sticks today. I'll watch sixteen-year-old Bibi in the garden of our house in the countryside (more on which in due course), galloping like a horse, the lawn chairs strewn in a circle as obstacles. She says she's practising mentally for her riding competition, and perhaps it's why she wins so often. She and the horse become blurred.

Ever since she's been able to walk, Bibi has been on a horse, which is odd considering she's grown up in a neighbourhood where the population density is the highest in Western Europe and where the only green is a sliver of grass near the Canal Saint-Martin. Regardless, she's always been drawn toward riding, partly because Anaïs's family are horse people (Hughes even played polo between rock concerts) and partly because pony clubs, as they're called, rank at the top of the list of parental aids when people ask me how we manage child care in France.

Pony clubs have saved my life on numerous week-long vacations I hadn't thought to organise ahead of time. In fact, pony clubs are babysitters, timeouts and cocktail parties for millions of French parents. Because they're not very expensive, they're everywhere in France, even in Paris, where you can ride your bike to either the Bois de Vincennes or, in our case, La Villette in the Nineteenth, and within minutes' walk amidst hay and stables while you answer email on your phone and your kids learn to ride. Classes run twice a week, and it's during these times that I've watched other parents network and gossip and discuss school and camps and strategise about whatever else is needed to survive French society. I must admit, it's worked for me, too. The woman who translates my articles? Pony club. Our best friends in the Perche? Pony club. Bibi's first ninth-grade student internship? Pony club. In fact, this book could usefully be titled 'Everything I Needed to Know about France, I Learned at Pony Club'.

Bibi has since graduated from ponies to full-grown horses and she now stars on a team that competes twice a month and for a week in July, when half of France descends on the small town of Lamotte-Beuvron for the Championnat de France, the equivalent of the French Kentucky Derby. There, members of every pony club in the country jump obstacles and perform dressage while their parents walk through mud and work the connections they've been making since childhood.

Bibi stands out on her team, not only because she's the youngest, but also because she has the longest commute. While her teammates arrive by car or scooter from the posh neighbourhood of Neuilly-sur-Seine or the chic *banlieue* (suburb) of Saint-Cloud, Bibi takes the metro twice a week from the Tenth, with her riding helmet and whip.

If Bibi was a porcelain figurine at birth, Otto looked more like a shirtless boatswain. The moment I first saw him, there was no question of a *couveuse*. The incubators were all too small. Instead Otto's massive hulk hung over the sides of a wheeled tray, looking like a hooked tuna, his hands the size of oven mitts. We'd been hesitating between two names if the baby was a boy, Gustave and Otto, and now the choice seemed obvious.

'Otto von Sothen?' my dad said when he first heard the name of his grandson. 'Sounds like a damn James Bond villain.' It's true Otto's name is a mouthful. But it has such oomph to it, I wonder sometimes if he's destined for great things. There was a tenth-century Holy Roman Emperor, I tell him, and a Bavarian Otto who became the first king of Greece. There was Otto von Bismarck. Otto Preminger. 'And Otto Porter, Jr,' Otto now proudly adds, citing the name of the Washington Wizards' starting small forward.

Like Hughes, though, Otto's already going against type. He has three types of hair gel to give him a perfect Cristiano Ronaldo soccer star coiffe, and he's happiest when walking down the street in gym shorts, socks and shower sliders to buy a kebab, holding our mutt Bogart close at the collar to give off the air he's a pit bull. This is the same kid who managed to sneak a water-based decal onto his neck for his French passport photo.

Like Bibi, Otto started his career with Khadija, but he stayed with her until he scored a space in the crèche. After that, he'd attend school down the block, where he'd have the same teachers, the same curriculum and, since his parents never learned from their errors, he'd find himself on the same bench of shame that Bibi had endured. With Otto, we felt less anxious because we'd been through the process before. The only thing that worried us was that the boy refused to speak English. This was normal, I was told, for a child whose mother was French and whose father wasn't French – he was just confused.

By the time Otto turned six, a form of franglais had seeped into the house. Sentences like '*Why do the good guys dans les films always beat the wrongs?*' would be the norm. Gucci was pronounced *Gookie* and Calvin Klein *Calveen Klayne*. In the end, though, our blurred language wasn't Otto's or Bibi's fault. It was mine. I'd spoken to them too often in French, which is odd considering I don't speak it that well.

It wasn't until we were on vacation in the United States, when the kids were forced to sink or swim, that I could re-assure myself that both kids spoke English fairly fluently. But this only turned the knife more. 'Why won't they speak English to *me*?' I'd snivel to Anaïs, sensing there'd always be a distance between me and my children. Anaïs didn't want to hear my complaining. Only five days had passed since we landed in the United States, and already she'd had her fill of American kids.

Americans love to say they admire the French system, until they meet Anaïs, and realise it's much more hard-core than they thought. Anaïs is the walking embodiment of 'not to be fucked with'. She has no problem telling kids to disappear while the adults are having an *apéro*, and any form of whining is met with a 'Stop trying to make yourself interesting.' Once a friend of Otto's proudly proclaimed to Anaïs, 'I don't do the dishes at my house,' at which point she handed him a stack of dirty plates and said, 'Well, here's to new beginnings.'

During a long weekend with another couple, staying at a converted château in Burgundy, Anaïs and I were content to finally sit down for dinner with our friends in the hotel restaurant after settling the kids in bed. Unfortunately, this adult time lasted only half an hour, when Bibi and Otto greeted us at the table, having snuck out of their ground floor rooms to surprise us. American parents would either laugh at their children's cuteness or wonder how it was the two had managed to sneak out of their room (by the window apparently). Anaïs did neither. She simply lit up her cigarette and stared out at the restaurant, turning back to the table after two or three puffs to let Bibi and Otto know in no uncertain terms, 'You ruin everything.'

When we visit the United States, our friends' children, you can tell, aren't sure what to make of this woman with her cigarette and glass of wine. They're not used to someone with an accent and a husky voice, telling them, 'If you can't arrive at a choice for a movie in the next five minutes, then there will be no movie. *Un point c'est tout!*' (She says the last part in French to make it sound more intimidating.) Anaïs has made a name for herself even inside France, to the point where my school-gate friend Fred christened her the *méchante dame* (the mean lady). The title couldn't be further from the truth. Anaïs is as loving and nurturing as they come, but for her, children crave limits, and there's nothing more borderline cruel and abusive than giving children the run of the place. Ironically, this makes my job easier, especially when it's my turn to restore order during a dinner. All I have to do is lean into the room and whisper to the kids, 'Do you want me to call the *méchante dame*?'

It wasn't until Anaïs began working on plays and operas abroad and outside Paris that I realised how much of the load she carried. With her absent, I was the constant chaotic mess of the neighbourhood, walking the dog to pick up groceries and paper for the printer before dropping by the school to let them know Otto had a dentist appointment for ... 'Wait, it was yesterday. *Merde!*'

Ironically, the ones who sympathised the most weren't fellow dads, but other mothers, which showed how macho France still is, despite all its crèche-ness and working moms.' Honestly, I admire you, John,' they'd say as they grimaced at their husbands, who glared at me as if I were some teacher's pet. These women didn't know the real story: that without Anaïs, we lived off Picard (the frozen gourmet supermarket) and that I'd sometimes go to bed before the kids, reassured that 'at least they ate well at school'.

Indeed, each day at school drop-off, I'd eye the menu Margaret posted on the door, amazed by the variety and balance. Filet of sole with *taboulé* – and peaches for dessert. *Saucisses de Morteau* and lentils with a side of puree (if you wanted it). The school puts such a premium on food, the head chef has an apartment across the street so he can arrive early and start making everything from scratch first thing in the morning. There were times when I was parenting solo that I considered asking Otto and Bibi to smuggle out some of their school lunches in Tupperware to eat that night.

For *collège*, which is what the French call senior school, starting at age eleven, we decided Bibi and Otto would go bilingual. Most schools that offer this are private, but a handful of state schools have a *section internationale* whose classes are composed largely of Anglophone kids. The snag is that they all have an excruciating entrance test, and then a fairly rigorous course load, which includes eight hours of English literature, history and geography on top of the normal French curriculum. But the idea of each kid reading *Catcher in the Rye* in English was too good to pass up. So we – or, rather, Bibi and Otto – jumped through the hoops.

Exams and workload aside, the other drawback with *internationale* was in Bibi and Otto leaving the familiar confines of our neighbourhood, and making a two- or three-change metro ride journey each morning. They had to leave the house at 7.15 to be at class by 8am and, since the school didn't provide lockers, lug giant backpacks like sherpas on a crowded metro. Another change, about the time Bibi began *collège*, was that the famous *carnet de correspondance* became electronic, and we'd receive regular emails starting with *J'ai l'honneur de vous informer* and ending anticlimactically with *Bibi was late this morning*.

I can tell this suits many of the parents, who send out emails on a nightly basis asking not just about what homework is planned, but debating the answer to question five on the second page. I'm the opposite of these parents. I'm so impressed that Otto can write a four-page essay on Clovis, what do I care if his grammar's a bit off?

But, starting in *collège*, every grade matters, and the *we're all in it together* approach I had witnessed in *elémentaire* and *maternelle* is scrapped for a passionless culling of the herd. *Collège* is where the French public system shows its schizophrenia. The same schools that give dyslexic students extra time on the *baccalauréat* tests or hire an additional assistant when a disabled child needs help walking to class can also show a cold indifference to those students who skip classes or fail out. And the students surprised me, too. On one hand, they seem to lack school pride; there is no cheering for your home team, no inter-school rivalries, no prom. And yet, each year, they will organise protests called *blocus*, where they'll block the entrances and shut down the school as a way to bring attention to demands for smaller class sizes and even better school supplies. Any time Bibi comes home early saying school was cancelled because of a *blocus* I'm annoyed, while at the same time impressed.

These very students are at the forefront of a debate that's consuming France right now. In contrast to America, France's educational system makes up 16 per cent of the total federal budget – fifteen billion euros more than the military. And yet many in France feel it's not enough; that class size and school conditions and teacher pay can all improve, not to mention that the days should be shorter. As an American who's watched public education wither and die since the Carter administration, I want to tell these people, 'Be happy with what you have.' But that's the thing. They have what they have *because* they're not happy and because they're willing to speak up and block entrances.

When I visit my old private school in the US and see the sumptuous renovated football fields and flashy new wings alumni have contributed to, I compare that to the school Bibi and Otto have attended since crèche and think, 'Was all this floor-to-ceiling glass necessary?' And perhaps it is the case. Perhaps there's enough money for scholarships and teacher pay to go around. But, whereas my reflex once was to turn my nose up at anything free, I now judge anything private and high-end with scepticism, probably because my idea of quality has changed somewhat.

Our state paediatrician's waiting room doubles as his living room at night. And that's fine. I'm not looking for the meticulous and gadgeted. I'm looking for a good doctor. Same goes for school. Sure, I want Bibi and Otto to come home once and not complain that there's still no toilet paper in the bathrooms. But that same school took Otto's entire class to Brittany for a *classe de mer* (sea class), where students slept in bunks and studied tides and learned to sail catamarans for a week, free of charge. And they couldn't be blasé on the trip because they were joined by others who'd never even been to the ocean before.

Another of the critiques (with which I agree, up to a point) is that the school system is gruelling, and that France is slowly becoming a European version of Japan. Too much weight is given to grades and your child's score on the Bac, a one-shot test kids prepare four years to take. Countless French parents have told me that when their children hit university, they have trouble adjusting to the informality of discussion groups with professors. Since it's been drilled into them to take copious notes and not speak out of turn, the result often is reticent kids who know tons but who are afraid to jump into the fray. And this isn't just for Engineering or History majors, but even Drama students. One French actor told me he needed to take improvisational classes just to get him to the place where 'American actors are naturally'.

According to a recent study, French pessimism (which is 10 per cent above the world average) finds its roots in the educational system. Teachers, the study says, tend to lace commentary and grades with judgment, 'making students feel guilty for not knowing'. The result is students going to school with 'a fear of failure rather than a desire to learn'.

It's certainly true that when Otto and Bibi come back each year from their US summer camps, I can tell they've had a culture shock. Not just from the 'kiss, marry or kill' games they learned or the Gronk jerseys they suddenly want, but from all the positivity. Each admits it takes weeks to trust that their fellow campers and counsellors aren't bullshitting them. And, for about a month following their return, some of it sticks. 'Great job, Dad!' I'll hear when I take out the dog, or 'Dad, I'm glad we had this talk,' Bibi will say in a syrupy voice when I turn off the light for bed. By the time French school starts again, the cheeriness is usually out of their systems, and thank God for that.

In France, each child has a *carnet de santé*, a vinyl-covered captain's log of all their medical issues since birth – the doctor's visits, the vaccinations and the markings showing a gradual increase in height and weight. I stared at Bibi's *carnet* the other day while we sat in a doctor's office, thumbing through the pages, starting with her birth and moving toward the middle, where all the bronchitis scares and broken arms lay. When I looked up from the log, there was a French adolescent across from me, one who this time needed an X-ray of a sprained ankle. And there in the waiting room, amidst tons of future parents holding ultrasounds and looking on nervously – much as I had done years ago – Bibi turned to me, smiling, and spoke loudly in perfectly native French (just so everyone could understand): 'Papa, I promise. Next time I'll use protection.'

While those around us looked up from their phones to stare at us, and while I turned red, I realised this moment perfectly summed up my French parenthood. For all the refinement and sophistication and urbanity or whatever else I assumed parenting in Paris might throw off, there's also been an equal amount of humiliation and bewilderment, not to mention scraping and hustling and countless nights of *biberon*-giving, while James Earl Jones's 'You're Watching CNN' booms in the background.

Bringing up babies in France isn't chic. Well, at least my experience hasn't been. But now that the clay is dry, the sculpture's set and the cracks in the base will be for some shrink to sort out, I can look on the two masterpieces Anaïs and I and the French system have made and safely declare that parenting in France is not the slick, shiny car I built it up to be, but just a slow and durable junker – one I could never bear to part with.

CHAPTER FOUR

OÙ EST JOHN?

ONE OF THE SELLING POINTS that Anaïs pitched me (after shooting me in the neck with a dart gun and bundling me off to France to live the rest of my days) was that we'd have a lot of vacation time.

Why she was talking about vacation when Bibi was on the way, I do not know. She probably should have been pushing the free health care and day care we'd be getting, which far outweighed for me the lure of time off, something I assumed I'd be giving up anyway by becoming a father. The fact neither of us worked real jobs apparently had no bearing, either. To Anaïs, the long French breaks meant we'd no longer feel guilty about not working, as our whole country would be doing the same at least six weeks a year.

To me, a newly arrived immigrant without a job offer, a vacation felt unearned. I was in the throes of grocery shopping my life – tossing marriage, child and moving to a foreign country into the same basket, simply because that was the only way I could have made life-altering decisions like these: on the fly, not really knowing what I'm doing because half of it's in French anyway. In January, we'd found an apartment. By April we'd had our wedding, and in late Jun, Bibi arrived. Perfect timing, one of the French nurses remarked, to go on vacation in August.

That the French went on vacation a lot wasn't news to me. Street sweepers and taxi drivers, plumbers and waiters – every class took the mandated time off. What I didn't know was how seriously the French took *planning* their vacations, that it wasn't just a brain-dead national ritual, but a year-long project, one that required diligence, research and tenacity, not to mention a willingness to squirrel money away to pay for it, often forgoing frivolous pleasures like eating.

I learned the hard way my first few years in France that vacation wasn't to be trifled with, and if I'd listened to the fellow parents more at Bibi's school, I would have known the game sooner. When Bibi was in the local school, I'd built up a rapport with quite a number of said parents, a rapport similar to what I imagine fellow inmates share: although you may not have much in common, you occupy the same prison yard (the paediatrician, the pharmacist, the *boulanger*, the fish guy, cheese guy, all within a three-hundred-yard radius of each other), and thus have a peculiar bond. Thus, I knew Nathalie well enough to know I probably wouldn't ever invite her over for a dinner, but that I could bitch about other parents with her and complain to her if necessary. I also saw her much more often than my real friends.

'*Vous partez où?*' Nathalie asked me as we stood outside of school waiting for our kids to come out.

I responded straight-faced to her question with 'The Monoprix,' assuming she was asking me where I was going to *now*, as in at that moment, the Monoprix being the local supermarket.

Her nervous laugh indicated a tinge of worry on her end, because any parent in France who doesn't have a vacation planned when school's about to recess is not just neglectful, but also possibly abusive.

'No, I meant *vacances*, silly. You're not going to leave them at the Centre de Loisirs, are you?'

The Centre de Loisirs is the programme every French state school offers kids who don't go away for vacation, which is a great idea in theory, especially for parents like me who don't have their own *Mamie* or *Papi* at their beck and call, as so many of our French friends do. I'm sure it's not that bad, but our kids have painted it in an *Oliver Twist* light, a place where you're handed pieces of bread and kept in a dark room and forced to play broken games of Connect 4.

The Centre de Loisirs is, in fact, a handy deterrent when they act up: 'That's it! You're off to the Centre this break!' I've found myself screaming when they crack my iPad. It's then that their faces turn white. 'No! Papa, please! *Pas le Centre!*' they beg in French, thinking that will make them more endearing. '*On sera sages, on promet!*' (We'll be good, we promise), they blubber, offering to paint the living room on top of getting straight A's.

So imagine Nathalie's surprise when I couldn't tell her where I was *partir*-ing to; not because I'd forgotten, but because I didn't realise there was vacation coming up.

But how could I? Where I grew up, nobody vacationed in the middle of February *for two weeks* – a holiday created in France to support the ski industry in towns that rely on the tourism. Nobody went away over Halloween – again *for two weeks* – for something called Toussaint (All Saints). A week here, two weeks there, three weeks in August and loads of three-day weekends that pop up throughout the French calendar. May has four, sometimes five 'long weekends' in one month, which is why I've coined it 'the New August.' If it's not May Day, it's Victory Day. If it's not Pentecost, it's Ascension. And, if you want to get freaky, you can take your RTT (sick days or off days – I don't know, I've never qualified) on a Thursday or Tuesday and *faire le pont* (make a bridge) to, *poof!* a four-day weekend or even five-day weekend, depending on whether there's a strike planned the following day. All of this thanks to France's dubious honour of being a pro-labour Catholic country that has fought in two world wars, and is not afraid to push back with an employer.

Nathalie was making small talk, sure, but it was French small talk, and although her question was put to me as an icebreaker, there was an angle to it. Vacations are not just times to relax in France, they're subtle status symbols. Nobody gives a shit if you have a BMW, but a dad who trucks his kids off to the Atlantic coast island of Île de Ré for a week gets a second glance.

'No,' I promised Nathalie. 'Bibi won't be doing the Centre,' knowing full well the sign-up period had long passed anyway. 'I'm not sure what we'll do,' I said, slowly getting annoyed at both her and myself. 'If anything, we'll just use this time to stay in town and get closer as a family.' I smiled and looked at my phone, wanting her to disappear.

The future favours the bold, and French vacations favour those who plan. In a country with 0.1 per cent annual growth, demand is high and supply is tight. I realise now why the French treat *soldes* (sales) invitations like concert tickets, willing to stand at the door hours before opening, and why purchasing winter term school supplies needs to be done in June – meaning my kids have never had the cool Eastpak backpacks, but instead the left-over *Dora the Explorer* ones they're too old for.

In the States, there is always a last-minute spot on an Amtrak train or a house in the Poconos to rent if it really comes down to it; the Hertz will have that Opel tucked away somewhere on the lot and, if you are up against the wall, you can always call the Great Wolf Lodge. But in France, there are no Cinderella stories.

Countless times, I've called rental agencies or hotels only to hear there's no vacancy. But, whereas you'd expect a simple '*Non*' and click, the French like to turn the knife.

'April of *this* year?' they'll ask.

I could imagine them hanging up to recount my pathetic call to their co-workers. 'A guy called this morning, foreign accent, asking for a room … get this, for next week!' They'd all roar, I'm sure, until their thoughts would turn to my kids and the wretched predicament the two of them faced – never having a planned vacation, never knowing ahead of time that a three-day weekend was about to drop, standing there in front of school in their *Go Diego Go* fanny packs.

You can find last-minute vacation offers in France, but they are always suspect. They're like the last remaining roast chicken you see turning on the rotisserie. Why is it still there? Is it uncooked? Was it dropped? There's something too good to be true when you find a house available in France the week before you're meant to leave. You get the feeling you don't have all the information. Maybe April's particularly rainy in Strasbourg, or there's weirdly no snow in Chamonix in March, or maybe that charming house in Brittany actually had a murder in it.

To say our vacations were awful our first few years in France would be an understatement. There was always a tragic element to them: broken collarbones, horrible storms, lost luggage. Sure, this could have happened to anybody, but the fact these mishaps were routinely visited upon us meant we were doing something wrong.

I probably should have realised that unorganised people with young children and little sleep and not much money, rushing to destinations they'd done little research on, were doomed to fail. I was selecting random places in France only because there was a vacancy, and a two-bedroom with a garden featured. The fact that I couldn't even find these places on a map didn't matter to me, which, in retrospect, made me the equivalent of a French person living in America saying to his wife, 'Look, honey, there's a nice cottage in ... where's Allentown, Pennsylvania?'

And, to make matters worse, Anaïs could never tell me where these places were! She'd lived in Paris her whole life. She's smoked since she was thirteen, and she's such a city kid, I think she may possibly be part rat. One would have thought a French native would know the basics, but in Anaïs's case travel outside the *Périphérique* (the Parisian ring road) was limited to a school trip to Mont-Saint-Michel. That and Spain, where her grandparents had lived. Anaïs and her sister would join them each summer at a villa on a lake in the mountains near Madrid, heading to the airport the day school let out, to return only the night before classes started in September. For Anaïs, Paris was a gulag you lived in five-sixths of the year so you could go to Spain for two months and waterski on an artificial lake with your cousins while parents and grandparents and aunts and uncles had cocktails and talked around stone tables under pine trees until 3am.

I, on the other hand, was just continuing a tradition handed down by my parents, who themselves were Griswold-esque in their preparation and execution. As a child, I thought everyone capsized Boston Whalers in Cape Cod (which is apparently hard to do) or had their luggage stolen in Budapest, or unwittingly brought poison ivy into China. And moving to a country where vacation was apparently respected and perfected and where I as the family patriarch would organise it all wouldn't change that.

My rookie error was trying to stay in Paris one summer, naïvely thinking I'd beat the French at their own game. When everyone else left, we'd have Paris, a beautiful city in its own right, to ourselves. But if you spend an August here, something dark happens to you. You die a bit inside, and you simulate, if only for a brief moment, what life would be like following a biological attack. After July 15 the Left Bank – or what used to be the Left Bank – becomes an annexed protectorate of Wichita, Kansas. You drift by hordes of Reebok-wearing tourists looking for the *Louv-ray* on your way to or from another closed café, wondering where you went wrong in life. And in the places that aren't very touristy, my neighbourhood, for example, everything is so closed you might possibly starve to death.

Plus, my wife finds the touristy things creepy. She had not only never been up in the Eiffel Tower, she had never been to its base. For her, Paris isn't supposed to be sunny and breezy. It's supposed to be trench-coat damp and foreboding, at least during the months she was used to being in Paris. Taking a tour down the sun-filled Seine on the Bateaux-Mouches in August wasn't a Parisian thing at all for her, it was a Vegas thing. 'But at least with Las Vegas,' she remarked as I took a cheesy photo of her half-smiling, 'we'd know that eventually we could come home to Paris. Whereas now, we can't come home, because we're already home.' It made more sense in French.

Unlike me, Anaïs didn't care where other people were holidaying, nor did she feel angry they had grandmothers who could lighten the babysitting load during these obscene amounts of time off, or that they always had stuff planned and things booked. Because another thing Anaïs isn't is jealous, which makes for a good balance, because that's all that I am. Whereas she'll be polite listening to someone recount their trip to the Dordogne region, deep down, aside from hoping they had a good time, she really doesn't care. Whereas I do, and, much the same way a motivated social climber will mimic an accent he thinks is 'proper', I slowly began asking people exactly where the Dordogne was and what they packed for those three-day weekends and when they looked for houses for the summer, trying to find patterns and links that would help me crack the code on how the French pulled off vacations.

'Well, we went with Raphael and Eleanor to Corsica last year, and Antoine and Sophia and their kids joined us,' I heard over drinks before dinner. 'We skied in Megève this winter with Thérèse and her kids, and my mother joined us with her boyfriend, and Thibault came down for a few days,' I noted at the sandpit, where Bibi was stealing the shovel off another kid because I, of course, had forgotten to bring hers.

The common thread throughout all this was there was never just a 'we', meaning the immediate family. There were always friends involved or cousins or neighbours or fellow parents from school. And now I know why. If you have six weeks of vacation and a slew of three-day weekends and a mid-range salary, whether you like it or not, you're going to be vacationing *en groupe*.

Our holidays had been abject failures because we were bucking the trend, trying to go it alone. What if we became fully French and vacationed like the rest of them, meaning with friends? It would be cheaper. Others more talented than us could plan. Plus, it couldn't be worse than what we were doing already, could it? Could it?

The French start their summer vacation planning ritual on the 1st of January. It's almost as if they chant the New Year's countdown – 4–3–2–1 – and start to look at farmhouses in Provence as the champagne pops. They do so because they know they're about to enter the months of January and February, which are so dreary, you need to live vicariously through the photos of a vacation rental, just so you don't shoot yourself.

I should have known during a dinner with friends a few weeks into the new year that the vacation talk being bandied about the table would become more serious once we retired to the salon for a *digestif* (the ceremonial post-dinner drink). I normally ignore the conversation during these kinds of sit-downs simply because I'm often too drunk to talk. But this time, I could still feel the warm glow of the music and the faces around me.

As the laptop was moved to the coffee table and we all snuggled around the couch looking like an impromptu key party, our group began sketching out houses to rent. Greece was in play for an early part of the primary, then Spain made a run, but as choices were vetoed and prices compared, we coalesced around Italy, and the long shot of Umbria. It wasn't so touristy as Tuscany, and it was cheaper. The house was bigger, and it featured one of those infinity pools overlooking the hills.

What I didn't know, though, was that by merely looking at the photos and parroting phrases like '*c'est génial*' and '*pourquoi pas!*' and '*cool!*' and '*super cool!*' I was signing a moral lease that bound us to these people eight months down the road, where we'd find ourselves driving from Rome into the hills of Umbria.

So that summer, as the von Griswolds (Anaïs, Bibi and me) comfortably made our way through the Umbrian countryside, Herr Patriarch at the helm, lush chestnut groves and elm forests, and sweet wafts of lavender streamed through the sunroof. The Italian heat was dry and made crisp by the sound of cicadas. And, as far as the eye could see, the ochre hills pitched and rolled, while the cypress trees that lined our road stood green and upright like soldiers saluting us.

I didn't realise at the time, but I probably should have been flooring it.

I say this because I didn't know that on *vacances* your bedroom isn't decided by who draws the longest straw, or who pays the most, but by the time-honoured agreement of first come, first served. And I learned this only upon arrival, when nobody was there to greet us. Well, they were, but not in the house. Instead everyone was lounging by the pool, already unpacked and lazily chatting away. The move-in time had been a mere twenty minutes ago.

On our way to the last available room, we passed the airy and cool ones already taken on the lower floor, those with the big windows, which overlooked the pool and the hills behind it. Our friends looked impressively settled in. Laptops were open, clothes were strewn everywhere (on purpose, I'm sure) as if to say, 'Look, I can't just pick up and switch rooms with John and Anaïs now, I'm installed.' I even saw a photo hurriedly tacked to a wall.

The room that was to be ours, on the other hand, was up a long flight of stairs and at the end of a hall, and was dark and stuffy, thanks to its one window being covered in thick ivy. 'You have great shade! I'm jealous,' our friend said as she left us to gripe. I kept a stiff upper lip while unpacking, knowing full well there's nothing worse than a guest who makes a fuss the first day. Plus, there wasn't time to stress about the room being an oven, as there were tons of people downstairs whom I hadn't formally met.

I'd met some of them, of course, but not all, because what's written in the fine print of French vacations is that you not only vacation with friends, you vacation with *their* friends as well. This can be good and bad. Sometimes the people are cooler than your actual friend, which gives you the option of upgrading. Other times, they're so awful, it makes you question not only your friend's taste in people, but also whether you're the exception or the norm.

And then there are surprise guests. It's not until you're in the car driving to the destination that you'll receive a text explaining that someone's mom is set to 'pass through'. She's not staying 'the whole time', they'll explain, just ten of the fourteen days. Again you'll shrug it off, because you don't want to be the guy who complains about someone's mother showing up. Plus, seventy-year-old French mothers are more spritely than their American counterparts. They probably saw the Stones live, they might own a Mapplethorpe and you can talk about sex in front of them.

Our friends from that initial dinner were Elizabeth and Stan. Both worked corporate jobs, which I assumed would be a benefit, because I didn't see vacationing with skimping artists as much of a vacation. Better, I thought, to relax with people who hate their jobs enough to really want to go all out during their earned time off.

Exept there was actually one artist. Bashir, a painter and sculptor who was so fit I called him 'the sculpted sculptor'. Then there were the singles – François and Simone. No, they weren't a recomposed couple, but maybe that's what French vacations are for, I told myself. Maybe we were witnessing the beginning of a long relationship and it would be thanks to a small gesture on my part, such as allowing François to sit next to Simone during dinner the first night, that would put in place the fireworks.

By the way, and this cannot be underlined enough, we were the only ones with a child in tow. Four-year-old Bibi was embarking on her first real vacation, too, and it turned out she'd end up being the only friend I could count on during our stay.

Our infinity pool sat flat as a mirror the first day, the raft slowly drifting from one end to the other, and as the sun set over our house, it gradually cast a long azure shadow on the valley below. I didn't see this, of course, because I was at the supermarket, then at the cheese guy in another village, then at a ham guy in another village five kilometres away. We were five or six adults cramming into a small car and then into small shops, half of us with our hands in our pockets doing nothing but looking like bored kids on a school outing. Once the food was gathered, the mission was to drive to another village to find the right wine and, since the market that sold the fish was closed on Sunday, it was decided we'd come back the next day, because why else would you go to Umbria if not to drive around in a clown car looking for tuna?

For the French, the first twenty-four hours of vacation are reserved for the food shop. The food and the menu are so serious and, if you're not huddled in long debates about who wants what on the menu that week, you're party to a soul-crushing slog through the badly lit cold aisles of chain supermarkets, only to find you don't buy the same things.

'You eat *that* bread, John, really? Do you know how much gluten it has?'

'Cocoa Puffs, wow! Look what John gives his kid!'

Sometimes your French friends will come with recipes they've ripped out of *Elle* magazine. Other times, they'll want to get the lay of the land before deciding what to try. Mostly, though, it's climate-related: for winter, hearty dishes like a *pot au feu* (beef stew) or *rôti de porc* (roast pork) or the cholesterol-filled widow-maker *cassoulet*. In summer, lots of gazpacho, goat cheese mint salads, mozzarella and melons.

The French are naturally good cooks, I'll give them that. They're like friends who grew up with dads who were gearheads and can fix a lawnmower engine as easily as I can tweet. Although it comes naturally to most of them, though, the French can be a bit cocky sometimes, to the point where cooking restaurant-quality dishes isn't, in their minds, a matter of experience and years honed in the bowels of a restaurant, but more of time, as in if they had more time in the week, they, too, could do that *osso bucco de folie* (an osso bucco that will blow your mind). Vacations are a chance to get behind the apron and test their talents, which is great if you're the one cooking, not so great for the others who become de facto sous-chefs, prep-cooks or, in my case, kitchen hand/busboy. I can't tell you how many times I'd been relaxing by the pool only to hear 'O*ù est John?* He's supposed to beat those egg whites for me!' or, 'Did John get the charcoal ready?'

During our first dinner, I also learned that some in our group were dieting. Why you would choose vacation to do this, especially when you're in the heart of southern Italy, is beyond me. What it meant, though, was that the food, namely the gorgeous ham and mozzarella, plus all the delicacies I loved and all the talented French cuisine I dreamed of gorging myself on, would be rationed down to the gramme. And if the plate wasn't passed your way on the first helping, well, you might not even get a small serving.

The food rationing was also a warning shot for just how potent the notion of 'group' is with the French. If everyone is set on one course of action (say, rationing), you're expected to step in line.

'Why *can't* I, though?' I whined to Anaïs, wanting to know why I couldn't just unhinge my jaw and pack the food down my neck, while the others were dieting. '*C'est juste comme ça*,' she replied, while we went to the kitchen to find dessert (fruit). 'And anyway,' looking at my waist for a pause, 'it probably won't do you any harm.'

Over coffee and candlelight, it was announced with fanfare that there would be activities, too, but not the kind you find listed in a pile of brochures inside a laminated pouch on the dining room table, which the owner had left behind for us. No, the activities announced at our table were more organic ones, *ateliers* ('workshops'). And each *atelier* would be headed by, yes, one of us, depending on our respective talents and passions. Let me repeat this. On the first night of my first French vacation, I was told I'd be running a two-week workshop. The list I'd noticed thumbtacked to a corkboard in the entrance hall had been just that, the atelier listing, with the programmes written down next to the name of the *professeur*. There was an *atelier abdos-fessiers* (a snobby word for *crunches*) led by Elizabeth, plus an atelier *peinture* guided by Simone, an *atelier philosophie* (Spinoza followed by a question mark) was Stan's gig, and an atelier *théâtre* would be directed by Anaïs. Aside from the fear of having to act in a play, what stressed me the most was that it wasn't quickly apparent to me what *my* talent was.

Although they hadn't said it at the New Year's party, it was becoming clear this group had not only holidayed together before, they knew the proper order of operations: arrive at the house early to get the best room, write down your *atelier*, jump in the car for a six-hour food shop, and make sure you say *Grazie!* to other French people. (An aside: It turned out this group of French people was obsessed with speaking Italian to each other, and they'd apparently all learned it by pantomiming Roberto Benigni.)

I assumed the frantic pace set during these first few days was due in large part to the stressful schedule my friends had left behind in Paris, and I sympathised to a degree. It's not easy decompressing overnight, but it *was* doable. I know because I'd witnessed it first-hand on a trip to Jamaica once with my parents, where we came across a group of American vacationers who shared a skiff with us to a nearby island for a day trip. The group as a whole was nothing special, but their ringleader, a sequin-bikinied fifty-year-old with running lipstick, who'd stumbled onto our boat with a cheeky 'Step aside y'all, 'cause cap'n Reba's heeh,' was. Not only was she wearing one of those umbrella hats and carrying a travel coffee mug full of cheap margarita, she wore on her face a notion of fleeting time and an ability to shut down within hours of arrival, something my French Umbrian brethren didn't. Reba, I bet, had some hideous job at a Nashville vehicle dealership waiting for her, and she wasn't going to think of it once. As we pulled into shore at sunset, her slack-jawed sunken quip of 'Just slit mah wrists and let me dah' stuck with me as the proper motto for vacation etiquette.

The *atelier* I should have chaired was spoken English. That way I could have killed two birds with one stone. Throughout the trip, my fellow guests insisted on speaking English to me. Why, I don't know. If it wasn't *'John, is he in ze kitchen?'*, or *'Why not!'* interjected when it really wasn't the context, they'd corner me in the pool to recount to me their trip to the States. 'And then we drove cross-country on Route 66,' they'd start, the deathknell opening to any vacation story.

I've never driven on Route 66, and none of my American friends have either, and yet every French person I cross who's been to the States has. I've heard Route 66 mentioned so often, I've started to wonder if it's part of French territory that was never included in the Louisiana Purchase, if it stretches today from an Air France gate at JFK all the way through to the Grand Canyon and is inhabited only by actors hired to perform American clichés on a freeway driven by French tourists.

As Simone ground on about her vacation to *'le fahr west,'* I doggy-paddled to the lip of the pool, thinking about those poor actors, sweating in the heat, dressed as face-paint-and-feather-wearing Native Americans, their walkie-talkies clipped to their belts, comparing pension plans and catering issues, their conversation suddenly interrupted by a call telling them to get in place, that Simone's family of four from France was arriving in two minutes.

As fortune would have it, a heatwave was sweeping Europe that summer. Our nights were cruel, and thanks to the ivy covering the window, I lay in a soaked bed laughing at the folly of thinking I could ever sleep in this hellscape. It wasn't frustration as much as *wow! surprise*, the kind you have when you enter a sauna and you're fascinated by how inhuman it is.

I left Anaïs to her denial upstairs and spent our first week solo on one of the couches downstairs, which made things only partly bearable. My initiative was seen as peculiar by the others, if not a bit precious. 'What, can't John live without his little AC?' they needled Anaïs. Ironically, I had dreamed about AC the previous night, and the dream put me in a blinds-drawn hotel room in an anonymous Charlotte Radisson, soulless and freezing – a place I'd always imagined to be the nadir of American travel, but which now I gladly would have traded for.

On French vacation, there's no chance of sleeping in. I'd awake on the couch to a commotion in the kitchen made by early risers already fixing a giant tray the French call a *plateau,* which holds tea, coffee, bread, butter, cheese and jam for everyone. The *plateau* is a sort of dinner bell for French breakfasts, and its preparation is the signal that everyone is expected, once again, to eat and be together.

As far as I was concerned, the *plateau* could have been a bucket of bait. Small chitchat with people pre-coffee I find almost impossible, probably because my normal mornings usually involve a quick vomit followed by two espressos taken in complete silence in some dark corner as I grow back my human skin.

For a few mornings I kept my distance, scurrying up to my room after folding up the couch, telling them that 'I need to help Bibi put together that Lego horse stable she's been wanting to build.'

Bibi, I found out early on, hated *plateau* as much as I did. She was used to our laid-back style in Paris, which included baby bottles and cereals and croissants and coffee all served up in our bed each morning, an activity she called *le camping*. For the rest of her meals, Bibi had been raised like every other angelic French child, to be attentive and polite at the table, but mornings were different, because her parents, who hated mornings, were different.

Now in Umbria she was finding out she was expected to eat breakfast downstairs with everybody else *à table*, and there wouldn't be any *camping*.

'*Pourquoi?*' she asked, looking at me on the verge of tears.

'Because.' And I flashed her that unsettling smile Jack Nicholson perfected in *The Shining*. 'Because we're *en vacances*, that's why,' I said, my weird grin frozen in place.

Sure, it might have been cruel, but it was the cold unvarnished truth and, when I turned to leave, I sensed I'd won an ally.

'Well, I hate *vacances*, then,' she pouted.

'Me, too, dear. Me, too.' I hugged her.

My absence at *plateau*, in the grand tradition of French mockery (one that tends to isolate and humiliate the individual) was noticed. 'Where is our American?' they'd ask Anaïs as the *plateau* passed, loud enough for me to hear them through the ivy.

The Breakfast Club, as I called them, would then all wash dishes together and hit the pool. But there were never any calm laps or quiet float time. A net was brought over from the garage and a volleyball game would start up. I tried to sleep, but the bink of the ball, followed by a splash, then an '*Ohh – trois zéro!*' was hard to ignore. And, amidst the splashes and the yells – all of this at 9am – there was the announcement, 'One more game, and then we're off to food shop!' which was met with a sort of childish group response of '*Ouiiii!!!*'

Staring at the ceiling in my hot coffin, the lure of the cool water was too strong, and before long I found myself joining them. But what started as simple back-and-forth lobs soon morphed into a game, and, although I was a novice, my unorthodox serve turned out to be very effective. Before I knew it, the game had ramped up to become serious, and Bashir, the token artist who was somehow more fit than the rest of us, the one who'd taken the first and largest room upon arrival (although he was single), suddenly flashed in anger, which I found flattering, only because it meant my serve was baffling him. When his teammate François started bitching about meaningless points, their anger became mine, and soon I was flopping around the shallow end, trying to save the ball at all costs, spiking on a frail Simone, taunting the other team with wide eyes, all with the goal of beating Bashir's ass. Not because he'd taken my room and brought his own stress into my vacation, but because I wanted so badly just to be able to ask him at tomorrow's *plateau* if he planned on hosting his annual 'How to lose gracefully in volleyball *atelier*'?

The pool excitement soon made me hungry, though, and while the others were resting (for the first time) on their chairs following the game, I darted into the kitchen on wet feet and in a dripping bathing suit to raid the fridge. Normally this wasn't allowed, because no snacking is an unwritten rule on French vacations, and in French life for that matter, but the urge was too great. Halfway through pawing some mozzarella and cutting wedges of tomatoes, I heard footsteps, which forced me to shove the tomatoes in my mouth and, sadly, the mozzarella down my bathing suit. It was Elizabeth, who'd come to fetch water for the group, and I could tell she sensed something was up, probably because I looked odd standing there in the nook of the kitchen counter, my legs crossed like an adolescent hiding a joint.

'We'll be leaving for the village in a couple of minutes, if you want to get ready,' she said in a parental way. I nodded and smiled *oui oui* with a closed mouth and, since bathing-suit mozzarella should never be put on bread, I then inhaled it like a Jell-O shot and changed clothes for another two-hour shop.

I suspected this French obsession with being together on vacation existed, but not to this degree. I'm not sure if it's the ingrained notion of *République* they learn at school or if it comes from the socialist *colonies de vacances* (summer camps) they attend as children in July, camps that are so team-oriented and group-centred you're practically attached to your fellow campers by a harness. But the more my housemates wanted to be together, the more I wanted to be alone, and by the second week, the impromptu *atelier* I'd created could have been called 'Find hiding John'.

'*Où est John!*' became a group-rallying cry, because John, it seemed, was always needed for some pool game, some *boules* contest right before dinner, or a karaoke singalong of French seventies music. And, the more they looked, the better I hid. There were 'jogs' in the morning just so I could actually be by myself. There were fake long calls from the United States, just so I could play games on my phone, and long stints with Bibi either playing 'hide from the evil adults' or in the pool fake-teaching her how to swim just so I didn't have to hear the minstrel Italian being spoken on the terrace.

In order to escape, I stole away to the furnace called our room, where Anaïs was seated on the bed. I flung myself down, screaming into my pillow like a grounded teen. If you were downstairs you probably couldn't hear a thing, but if you were next to the bed, or if you had your ear to the door, you'd catch a muffled guttural hurl coming from the room, a sort of 'John's here, you fucking assholes! Fucking try and find me!'

'Oh, stop exaggerating. Look at you! You're going to get hot again!' Anaïs would scold. She had been oblivious to much of the horror I'd faced these past days, perhaps because, as a French person, she found most of it quite normal. That or maybe she assumed anybody after two weeks could come off as *pénible* (annoying). Anaïs's father often repeats a proverb attributed to Benjamin Franklin, 'Guests are like fish. After three days, they start to stink.' He usually tells us this on the fifth day of his stay at our apartment.

That night, on my mat during the nightly yoga atelier, as I sat in crow pose staring at the same laptop we'd used on that fateful New Year's Eve, now transformed into a screen to project *Yoga for Dummies*, I realised the celebrated French vacation I'd been led to believe was so awesome was kind of overrated.

It was decided our last night together would be 'American night', which meant we'd speak English all day and eat American for dinner, and, of course, yours truly was named cook. I accepted the nomination, only because I didn't want to confirm everyone's preconceived notion that Americans suck at cuisine. Plus, by choosing to do smoked barbecue, I'd be able to avoid all group activities planned that day with the excuse that someone had to keep an eye on all the ribs. And there, under a tree in the shade, I enjoyed a bag of crisps and a beer that I'd asked Bibi to smuggle to me. And as the hours passed, I'd routinely 'test' the ribs every hour, letting the sauce run down my stomach.

A soothing calm drifted over me. I'd finally found my sweet spot, and when we said our goodbyes over the *plateau* the following morning, I wasn't even angry any more at my friends for having hoodwinked me into French vacationing with them. I accepted them for who they were: people I'd gladly hang out with ... in Paris.

And as the years passed and we vacationed with other French people on different French holidays at different French locales, I began to realise my trip to Umbria was not an outlier but part of a general trend: one of skiing destinations two hundred miles away that take thirteen hours to drive to because of biblical traffic; a friend's house in Burgundy in the fall with no heat, whose kids your kids hate; or a wine-tasting trip to Bordeaux, whose vineyards don't even grow the wine you are drinking.

What Anaïs should have told me when she brought me to France years ago was that, at least for six weeks a year, we didn't have to feel guilty, because we, too, could skimp and cook, and hump bags of dirty laundry and truck bottles of half-finished olive oil all around the country with people we didn't even necessarily like on half-assed vacations we didn't really want to take.

On that Tuscan *vacance*, we returned a day before the *rentrée*, the ceremonial French back-to-school period, and in front of the school, while Bibi hugged her friends and scanned the Scotch-taped pages of the front door to see who her teacher would be for the year, the parents hung back and caught up on, of course, what else?

'*Alors? Vous êtes partis où?*' ('So? Where did you take off to?'), Nathalie asked. And as I began describing my first *real* French vacation, the photoshopped Instagram version, with great friends and food and 'lots of stories to tell', I could see the gears of her mind were already turning.

'Well, you sound like just the kind of people we should go on vacation with!'

And while she told me about the dinner she was organising that weekend to plan for next year's trip, extending an informal invite to *you know who*, I found myself backing away, ever so slowly, subtly looking over my shoulder for the one lifeboat I could count on to save me from all this French vacation.

'Bibi... Bibi?... BIBI!'

CHAPTER FIVE

LETTER FROM THE NO-GO ZONE

THE EVENING WE CLOSED ON OUR APARTMENT, Anaïs and I visited our future space with a bottle of champagne and some drawings sketched on napkins. And there in the upstairs bathroom, while we discussed (like all good *bobos* – *bo*urgeois *bo*hemians, as the French say) the pros and cons of installing matching sinks and a walk-in shower (a style the French call 'an Italian douche'), I spotted from our window a man sprinting down the street chased by another man with a brick. Since I didn't want the new-car smell of home to wear off just yet, I chose to assume the men in question were up to something nobler than what it seemed. Maybe the tall one had botched the taxi reservation and was running ahead to catch the driver, his buddy trailing behind with the pound cake they'd just baked. Perhaps the two were training for that restaurant race they have in Paris, where waiters run down the street weaving in between tables holding trays above their heads – the brick simulating the tray and the lead runner setting the pace.

A lot of my friends in the States refuse to buy it when I tell them that our neighbourhood's rough. They don't need to say it. I can see it on their faces as they stare back at me over beers. Sure, in large part their reverence is a way to butter me up before they ask to crash at our place for a week in spring, but deep down I honestly think they believe the myth of Paris is mine. So when Fox News blared that my Paris neighbourhood was a 'No-Go Zone', in 2015, that roving marauders had taken to the streets and imposed Sharia law, I felt oddly vindicated. No, my neighbourhood wasn't a 'caliphate of Paristinians', as some pundits claimed, but it wasn't a cakewalk, either. And it surely wasn't the place I imagined myself living when I first arrived, the one with the nineteenth-century Haussmannian facades and tree-lined boulevards and manicured parks where you can sit below a two-hundred-year-old willow, not realising your bench was actually a sculpture by Rodin.

Much of my vision at the time was nourished by the film *Amélie*, whose first cinema screening coincided with my arrival in France. The small-budget film that followed the life of a young woman discreetly controlling the lives of those around her went berserk at the box office, giving France its personal *Star Wars* moment and me cinematic inspiration. And, while there were some who critiqued the film, claiming its depiction of Paris was 'cliché ridden', even 'reactionary', and harkened back more to Vichy than to Edith Piaf, I was smitten. For me, Amélie's character didn't look like a collaborator at all. She wore her hair like Anaïs and walked and talked in accordion-playing Montmartre streets, waving to café owners and helping old ladies cross the street. No, she didn't really work and, like the characters in *Friends*, lived in an apartment she obviously couldn't afford, but who cared? She had the Parisian life I wanted.

The one hitch was that I was no longer a single twenty-five-year-old like Amélie and nor was Anaïs. In fact, she was seven months pregnant at the time, and the soon-to-be three of us living in a two-hundred-square-foot studio didn't strike me as charming. Montmartre prices (thanks in part to *Amélie*) had skyrocketed, so we soon found ourselves looking for larger places in other neighbourhoods, one being the Tenth, which was almost next door, and as Anaïs reminded me, it, too, had served as a backdrop for a couple of scenes in *Amélie*.

Although only three metro stops apart, the Tenth and Montmartre are starkly different, probably because they're separated by Barbès, Paris's quintessential Arab neighbourhood. If you choose to make the fifteen-minute walk east down the mount, you'll gradually notice a change not just in the inhabitants, but in the makeup of businesses along your way. Antique stores, upscale real estate offices and trendy cafés give way to mint tea rooms with dominoes players camped out at the sidewalk tables, Arabic wedding dress boutiques, Bollywood video stores and Western Union money transfer bureaus flashing Algeria and Morocco currency rates.

We'd been briefed by people that the Tenth was a bit '*chaud*' ('dicey'), due to a reputation it earned in the 1990s as a haven for drugs. But how bad could it really be, I wondered? Having lived in Brooklyn and East Harlem, I wasn't about to be intimidated by Paris. I mean, *please*. I'd been held up at gunpoint on 117th Street and scammed in Brooklyn by a man who tossed flour on me on the way to the subway one morning. I settled quickly with the scammer, paying him to leave me alone so my neighbours didn't pass me on the sidewalk covered in white powder, a stranger yelling in my face at 9am, 'But who's going to replace my stash!'

No. The Tenth wasn't quaint, time-honoured Montmartre, but it wasn't Gary, Indiana, either. There weren't bulletproof bodegas and vacant lots; just drab and boring storefronts and a bit more garbage. And, even if the brick-on-brick motif were true, I told myself, it only confirmed we'd followed Rule A of real estate success – buying low in a dodgy section at the right time. All we had to do now was wait like spiders for all the loser-come-latelies to arrive, so I could be that annoying holdover who brags when he points to the corner and says, 'You see that Kiehls store over there? It used be a crack house!'

And this was the narrative I'd hold to for years, despite the occasional glitches. The man climbing the wrought-iron fence of our backyard? Not a hopped-up junkie, just a neighbour who'd forgotten his keys. That woman I'd found dressing in the garbage room one winter morning? No doubt the custodian changing into her work gown, not a crackhead shitting in the drain. I was in Paris, the City of Lights, where the ether alone would raise my game in all fields. My kids would be the Cartier-Bresson-photographed icons of well-behaved *bébé* manners, and the beauty and sophistication of my surroundings would shepherd a new-found John toward dignified and continental grace.

Anaïs, on the other hand, was working off a different theme, one inspired more by industrial Brooklyn, where we'd met. She wanted space, which came in the form of our future apartment, a disinfected warehouse she'd stumbled upon while visiting an apartment nearby. The three-storey brick building was converting into lofts, two spaces per floor with each raw space delivered as is or, as the French poetically call it, *brut*. During our first visit, while I lingered on the third floor, trying to imagine how I could make the spread more *Amélie*-esque, Anaïs shouted up through the shaft that would be the building's future stairwell that she'd found the one with the most potential – the building's garage.

'This could be the salon,' she said as I stood next to her on a dirt floor staring at two Renault loading trucks. 'And upstairs *là bas*,' she pointed to what was maybe a twenty-five-foot ceiling of cables and ducts, 'we'll put in bedrooms.' Our apartment would be a bit *atypique*, as the French say. We asked for ceiling fans and wanted a 'play room', all of which the French contractors found bizarre and a waste of space. The more they became annoyed by our weird demands, the more they asked to be paid upfront *en black* (in cash). Funding your renovation partly in cash is standard in France. It's a way for contractors to keep their *charges* (employer taxes) down, and they're willing to reduce their prices some to make it happen. But this also meant my taking out wads of cash each Friday from the bank, the teller growing more and more suspicious each time I entered smiling, with a fake *bonjour*, to ask for five grand.

Also to keep costs down, we agreed to do a lot of the legwork for the contractors ourselves, which entailed my heading off to the Leroy Merlin, the Home Depot of France, looking for stuff I didn't know how to pronounce or use. *Rosace*, you may want to know, means 'kitchen tap ring'. Along the way, an order would be botched, which would slow the work, or I'd okay something I shouldn't have, because I didn't understand what the contractors were asking me on site. 'How high do you want these baseboards to be?' would be met with a simple *'Oui, merci,'* which generated a fatalist shrug on their end and a return to work. Things moved quickly this way, until Anaïs would arrive a few days later screaming with shock. 'Did you okay all of this? They said you did!' Feeling backed into the corner, I responded the only way I knew how. 'Well, they're lying!'

With hiccups like these, the renovation took longer than expected, which surprised nobody. All of our friends had their own stories; I'm convinced now that renovation is a French initiation ceremony all young couples must experience. We'd already sold Anaïs's studio in Montmartre to finance the work, so we were forced to move in before the renovation was complete. And there, after I carried Anaïs over the threshold, four-month-old Bibi crawled on the sanded cement floors looking as if she were veiled in nuclear fallout, her ash-covered face screaming for another bottle, me rummaging through another taped-up box looking for it.

Eventually, though, our apartment took on a true New York hue. We had our famous walk-in Berlusconi (as I called the Italian *douche*), the open kitchen. Bikes were in the living room. We had a tiny backyard with an Ikea rope swing. We even had the pretentious idea of hanging two clocks on the wall, one for New York and one for Paris. It was the kind of place whose owners you could easily be annoyed by. Even our friends were annoyed.

And the neighbourhood did improve. A movie theatre moved in nearby, and a park opened across the boulevard in the Nineteenth. We became close friends with some of the neighbours, and our kids would come and go in between apartments at all times of the day like travelling emissaries. I barbecued in our tiny garden with a beer, while Anaïs pushed Bibi in the swing, and if you took a close-cropped shot of us you might have pegged us for a young couple in Palisades Park, New Jersey.

As with all young parents, our life soon became enmeshed with the local school, a grey and beige monstrosity two hundred metres from our apartment. Every day at pick-up, I'd be struck by the odd bouillabaisse of parents whose children attended, a group I began calling the 'kale moms and veiled moms'. But what made this *mixité* so unique and Parisian wasn't just the Benetton ad of different colours and outfits standing side by side against the sidewalk pedestrian guard waiting for their kids to be let out, but the obvious economic variety of the parents, due not only to the strength of the Parisian state school, but also to a law that allows the city of Paris to make pre-emptive purchases of properties and land (which it does often) before they reach the open market. I'm sure other cities do this, but it's surprising to see in the centre of Paris where prices are so exorbitant. Having the right of refusal has allowed affordable housing to coexist in close proximity (next door) to private housing such as ours, and it's provided, I realise, a diversity that no longer really exists in American big cities. This doesn't mean the Tenth is one big melting pot and we're regularly having dinner with the Malian family down the street, but Bibi is friends with their daughter, and we do see them every day at the grocer's and at the school, and this proximity has led to a sense of camaraderie.

Another centre of gravity is the neighbourhood café, Le Cristal, where parents assemble post drop-off for a half-hour pause before heading off to work or back home to fake work. The *Café des parents*, as I called it, could be the idyllic setting for a reality TV series, only because there's a mix of mild flirtation, bitchy avoidance and outright disdain.

There are cliques and losers, jocks and nerds, a sort of parallel microcosm of the school sitting fifty metres away, but cast with people thirty years older.

There I met Rolland, a musician, whose side-project was shooting music videos of our fellow parents singing and dancing in various parts of the neighbourhood. Rolland took this beyond a hobby, and the *café des parents* was his casting couch. Recruits might casually agree to participate over a coffee on Tuesday, only to find themselves actually having to rehearse on Friday for a shoot on Saturday. That way, by Monday, everyone else from the Le Cristal could eagerly await a link in a mass email to see which couple embarrassed themselves singing Claude François or Joe Dassin. It was all fun and games until I found myself singing 'My Way' from a bridge overlooking the train tracks of Gare du Nord, and yes it is online and will be there long after I'm dead. Rolland's weekly videos were just one of the many events on our school's associated social calendar, which created a seasonal routine, no different from *les vendanges* (wine harvests) or apple picking.

In March, the neighbourhood would host the annual *carnival* (which often coincides with Mardi Gras), a sort of French block party à la Brazil where adjoining streets are blocked off and parents and neighbours and kids dance in the streets in costumes in a procession that slowly makes its way around the neighbourhood. Some walk on stilts, others toot trombones, and the confetti rains down from the neighbours' windows like snow. Anaïs, who spent hours helping the kids make a lot of these costumes, couldn't bear seeing the parade end so soon, so we'd throw an impromptu *carnival* after-party, parents and children filing in off the street with their face paint and cat tails, looking to milk the early *après-midi* for what it was worth. Some of the faces streaming in we'd see at birthday parties throughout the year. Some were complete strangers who'd never been to our house. One child was so impressed by the size of our loft he pulled me aside during the party with a pressing question. 'Sir, how is it you became a millionaire?'

'Hard work,' I told him. 'Lots of hard work.'

In June, there was the end-of-the-year school fair, called '*la kermesse*', which featured a student-performed concert and lots of pin-the-tail-on-the donkey style games. And at Christmas, there was ice-skating at the Piscine Pailleron, a ritual we started when I learned, to my horror, that French children open gifts on Christmas Eve. The way it works is that, after dinner, anyone who still believes in God (small few) heads to Midnight Mass, while the others linger around a table for an extra few hours waiting for them. Upon their arrival, when it's insanely late and children are too groggy to appreciate anything, *les cadeaux* are opened. How the French explain the whole Santa thing is anybody's guess.

Since I was having none of this, I began feverishly searching for alternatives, one being a rink in the bordering Nineteenth, the only place open on Christmas Eve. There we discovered others who hadn't bought into the Christmas Eve gift-opening charade – Orthodox Jews in yarmulkes, Muslims in headscarves – skating in unison to 50 Cent. Bibi and Otto flopped and fell and were too tired to even consider opening a gift on Christmas Eve. We haven't missed a year at the rink since.

In 2009, our school was rocked by news that students whose parents were undocumented immigrants, or what the French call '*sans papiers*', would be denied admission. Anaïs was furious, not only because some of the children from these families were Bibi's classmates, but because French law states that every child has the right to attend school regardless of his or her parents' legal status. The problem, Anaïs said, was that many of the families didn't speak French or were too intimidated to visit the precinct and challenge the ruling. She felt it was her *devoir* (duty) to become their liaison, and soon she was helping families navigate the voluminous paperwork needed to properly file for asylum or start the naturalisation process or simply obtain a stay of residence.

Within days, Anaïs was meeting *sans papiers* families at drop-off. They'd then head off to the commissariat or to our apartment to sort out birth certificates, demands for asylum or proof of employment. Within weeks there was a Malian family, who'd been evicted, staying downstairs in the guest room. There was a Sri Lankan family and an Egyptian family dropping by the house with stuff for us to photocopy. Once a week, Anaïs would update me and the kids over dinner on the 'Belonisse file', the 'Al-Adjur file' and, of course, '*les Soudanaïs*'.

Not to be outdone by his daughter, Hughes, too, began helping families in Montmartre, and a sort of inter-family rivalry sprang up, Hughes announcing he'd just bought a megaphone to protest while bragging that he'd helped an Iranian family secure papers. Anaïs graciously congratulated Hughes, but it was only after she hung up that I could tell she wasn't impressed. 'Iranians are easy,' she said, exhaling cigarette smoke. 'Their French is usually *pas mal*.'

And never once did Anaïs ask how I felt about all this. She just assumed I was okay with it, which I was, but I can't say I was comfortable. I'd never been the social warrior. And while Anaïs's parents participated in the '68 riots, throwing bricks and getting tear-gassed, my parents held a cocktail party while Reagan fired all air traffic controllers. Plus, I'd read that helping and sheltering *sans papiers* risked fine or imprisonment or expulsion. An alpinist in the Savoie region of France had been arrested for, get this, helping a refugee family find its way through the mountains. Did Anaïs understand her own husband could find himself on a one-way Air France flight back to his home? Maybe she wanted that.

But this wasn't about me and, after months of follow-ups and return meetings and finding translators, Anaïs's efforts would pay off. The families would receive their papers or at least a stay of deportation, and their children could continue to attend school. And, I admit, I was proud of my wife. That and a bit jealous of all the attention she was getting.

Before we knew it, streams of thanks showered down in our neighbourhood. Once, a Sri Lankan patriarch named Rashmi invited us to his restaurant in the neighbourhood. There he confided that he was happy to be a citizen now, or at least a green card holder, but France, he thought, needed to be tougher on jaywalkers. Jaywalkers to him were just as bad as criminals. 'You need to put them in jail longer, and definitely need to start caning them,' Rashmi told us as the samosas were passed and the Kingfisher beer flowed. Anaïs, I could see, was frowning but remained polite. She reminded Rashmi that caning was illegal in France, and many countries even saw it as a form of torture.

'Well, that's coming from someone who hasn't been caned.'

Rashmi told us he'd been caned in Singapore, and he felt the experience had put him on the straight and narrow. 'If I hadn't been caned, I wouldn't be here today.' For Rashmi, the person who'd caned him and the woman who'd helped to secure his papers had each taught him in their own way.

Rashmi wasn't the only one to quickly critique France once he was legal. Another family announced to Anaïs on the day of their written acceptance that 'The problem with France was all these *sans papiers!*'

'Admit it,' I said as we left their apartment. 'It has to make you burn a bit.'

'*Pas du tout,*' Anaïs told me. 'It just means they're already becoming French.'

And here we lived in this neighbourhood, where down the street old men smoked from hookahs called *chichas* and where Otto would bring home Ivory Coast *beignets* after having spent the night at his friend Najl-Adams's apartment across the street, where he'd even joined the family in Muslim prayer. We drank home-made Martiniquan punch made by Marie-Christine, whose son, Birham, was Bibi's first *amoureux*. During Ramadan, there was always a long table sitting out front on the street for those who'd managed to hold out all day. And if you had the courage to wait until 10pm to eat, you, too, could buy a plate right there on the sidewalk and scarf down with everyone else.

No, this wasn't *Amélie* by a long shot, but our community, I was learning, was uniquely Parisian. And despite all its improbability and idiosyncrasies, it always felt safe. It was America that routinely freaked us out, with its code oranges or anthrax scares or hurricane disasters or the *sniper*.

My friend Pierre had been visiting the DC area during the infamous sniper attacks in 2002 and had assumed it was a TV series, not a news event. From his perspective, anything that had graphic lead-ins announcing 'Coming up next, the *sniper*', or man on the street interviews with questions like 'What are your plans for tonight in light of *the sniper*?' had to be fiction. Pierre had been weaned on the straitlaced TF1 broadcasts at 8pm and the BBC-type delivery of French news on the radio. He wasn't versed in America's 24/7 cable news phenomenon, nor could he wrap his mind around how the news had become show business. The upside, he told me, was that he felt he had DC to himself during the panic, waltzing DC's street while everyone else cowered.

Each time I return to the States, I feel more and more like Pierre. There was a palpable aggressiveness to America that I just didn't find in Paris. It could have been the TVs overhead in the immigration line blaring on about *Hillary's email problem*. It could be the 'sir, what-is-your-reason-for-coming-here' syncopated delivery of the passport checker. Everything felt on steroids and by the book. The cops were huge. The atmosphere was military. Anaïs had to scrape her cornea on some eye machine. A solid three-week stay in August made me appreciate returning to France, where the energy was less in your face. There'd been terrorist attacks in Paris, mind you, but terrorism never seemed to preoccupy people.

Instead it was chill, and those improvised dinners we did on a Tuesday evening meant you could be spontaneous without the harsh consequences that always seem to accompany post-child impulsiveness. It also made the drift into adulthood seem so slow and graceful, you might even miss the fact you were getting old.

Yet, despite all of this sangfroid built into the French system, the terror attack on Le Carillon hit me hard, and that feeling of vulnerability I experienced at JFK immigration resurfaced. A slow fatalism sank in, a feeling that perhaps we were just at the beginning and not at the end of a series of horribleness, which took me back to the few weeks in New York after 9/11, when I expected to hear the other shoe drop: that the Holland Tunnel had blown up or that an Amtrak had been derailed on purpose or that cyanide was in the reservoir. In Paris, on weeknights, we'd often meet at Le Carillon for drinks after work and sit *en terrasse* while waiting for takeout from Le Petit Cambodge, the Cambodian restaurant across the street. It was a ritual done tons of times, with the kids in the stroller or running up and down the sidewalk, while we sipped wine and caught up with friends. The image of men rolling up in a car and firing Kalashnikovs into the crowd seemed as surreal as a plane hitting a tower.

Soon the vestiges of grief and anger seemed ever-present. There were candles and flowers and printed-out photos of the victims taped along the fences of the canal. There were headlines of *guerre* and *vengeance*. And, of course, there were emails from friends in the States bearing messages like 'We hope you're safe', or 'We're thinking of you' or 'We're all in shock' – messages that were meant to bring comfort and that I appreciated, but that I could never find the right response to, except for 'Thanks, dude.'

Suddenly, reporters from CNN and Fox and NBC camped out on the Place de la République, with their makeup and lights and bad hair. Their presence meant the Tenth had joined the ranks of places like Tel Aviv and Jerusalem or London in the 1970s, places where cafés and bars would remain open, but with a cloud of fear hanging overhead just like the gas lamps.

For me, Paris hadn't been attacked as much as the Tenth and Eleventh had. The terrorists themselves agreed. For them, our neighbourhood was a *zone grise* (grey zone), an abominable place in their mind, where Muslims and non-Muslims coexist on a daily basis. They could have attacked touristy locations like Saint Michel or the Pompidou Centre, denser populations like the Marais, symbolic places like the Louvre or the Eiffel Tower, but instead they chose us.

The Monday following the attacks, schools were open, and as Otto and his friends left our house I scrambled to the window like any crazy fearful parent, craning my neck out at the street to make sure everything was okay. Watching them head off, I couldn't help but wonder if the bill for the overgrown adolescence I'd been living had now come due. It was Paris's and my turn to stop being so naïve, to put away childish things and wake up to the howling wind that was blowing through the door, a door that the Tenth, because it was so inclusive and never suspicious and a bit ditsy, had always left open.

Within months, the city would morph into the fearful America I'd looked down on upon my return trips to the States. Otto would tell us at dinner that his class had practised tuck and rolls at school, their professor teaching them to hide under the desks and to lock the doors. Green-bereted militia would promenade our sidewalks in threes with machine guns, followed by a Humvee-type Jeep with the word *VIGIPIRATE* decaled on the windshield. We'd even learn that some of the terrorists had grown up nearby.

The John who assumed he'd one day be sashaying down a Montmartre street waving to his neighbours on his way to the market or bookshop was now at the Barbès metro embarrassingly racially profiling someone with a beard and tunic. The man in question had walked into the car holding too-large zippered shopping bags with Muslim prayers blasting in his earphones. I had panicked and stepped backward out of the carriage right before the doors closed.

And as the train pulled out, an immediate guilt mixed with anger, mixed with 'Fuck, I have to wait for another train', all hit me at the same time.

It also dawned on me that maybe I'd been play-acting as a sophisticate for years, dressing myself up as some noble urbanite, who maybe deep down liked feeling rich around those who were less privileged. Just look. We had a country house like all the other boujie cardigan-sweater-wearing couples in Paris, and Bibi was now going to school in a far-away arrondissement where people my age had grown out of their 'keeping it real' adolescence. There on the platform an odd cry leaked out, one that I guess came from frazzled nerves, comical irony and a touch of self-loathing. It was as if everything I'd been living and appreciating in France had just been twisted by a bad acid trip. My home was no longer what I thought it was, and neither was I.

At school, Anaïs noticed smaller things, too. Fatima, whose son Yassine was in Otto's class, was showing up to school now in a long black gown and matching hijab that covered her ears and forehead, something she hadn't worn before.

'Fatima, what's all this?' Anaïs asked in a tone you might use when someone shows up at the beach in socks. Anaïs felt she could ask because they knew each other well. She'd helped Fatima's husband, who was from Egypt, with his papers, and although the two weren't close friends they'd grown close in a sidewalk drop-off kind of way. I'd see them chat and wish each other *bonnes vacances* and even share a coffee on occasion.

'Fatima sera toujours Fatima' ('Fatima will always be Fatima'), she replied. 'Et Anaïs sera toujours Anaïs' ('And Anaïs will always be Anaïs'). But the way Fatima said it, Anaïs told me, repeating it in an almost mantra-like way, looking straight ahead toward the school door instead of back at Anaïs meant, indeed, that something had changed.

In the fall of 2015, Syrian, Eritrean and Malian refugees began appearing in our neighbourhood, because of its proximity to Gare du Nord, from which they hoped to eventually reach the UK by train. How they planned to do this was anybody's guess, but their haphazard plans looked almost Swiss compared to Paris's response to their arrival, which was a bad mix of denial, indifference and ultimately forceful removal.

For months, families would camp out in the basketball courts that sat in the middle of Boulevard de la Chapelle, the two-lane thoroughfare fifty yards from our apartment that links the north of Paris east to west. There, the migrants would hang laundry and sleep in makeshift cabins built of cardboard. Their numbers soon grew and, as they did, so did concerns over illness spreading, as no toilets or clean water were available to them. Children in diapers would walk in proximity to passing cars, lines would form for impromptu food handouts and, all this time, residents like us in the Tenth would continue our daily lives, heading off to work and stepping over them on our way to the metro, feeling almost numb.

The refugees did their best to keep their camp clean, but their numbers kept growing until police eventually arrived in the middle of the night with buses and cleaning crews to evict everyone, taking them away to God knows where. The basketball courts would be hosed down, barricades put in place, but that didn't stop the next wave of refugees from arriving the following week, starting the process all over again.

For the most part, the neighbourhood remained stoical, if not welcoming, during this time. Anaïs's theatre troupe performed a reading of James Joyce's *Ulysses* one night for those in the encampment. People volunteered to teach French. There were booths set up to help with medication, and all of this was done without the help of the city authorities, who still were operating under a 'hear no evil, see no evil' policy. The reaction of the posh Sixteenth Arrondissement, though, was noticeably different when it was announced that the city was opening a refugee centre in the Bois de Boulogne. The fact that this would be in the park itself and far from any housing didn't matter. Local news showed Sixteenth residents flooding their city hall meetings, old ladies pushing themselves through doors shouting at their mayor and the city to rescind its plan. And it worked. The refugee centre plan was scrapped.

In December, protesters calling themselves *Nuit Debout* (Standing at Night), a French version of Occupy Wall Street, arrived, looking to ally with the refugees. They'd routinely graffiti the street with *'Mort aux banquiers'* ('Death to bankers') and burn scooters for no reason other than to sow chaos. In March, *'les Sauvettes'*, a form of yard sales for gypsies, began appearing on the boulevard, too, providing gruesome scenes of people bartering used tubes of toothpaste for 2003 Nokia phones, all on a bedsheet they'd spread out in haste on the sidewalk below our window. Then, over the summer a *salle de shoot* (supervised heroin shoot centre) opened near the Gare du Nord, creating wandering zombies, high or desperate, kicking in café windows and rummaging through garbage cans while they waited for the centre to open.

Our world was on fire, I felt, and having grown up in DC's posh Georgetown district and attended a buttoned-up private school, I began wondering why the hell I was letting my kids grow up in such a place.

'That's selfishness,' Anaïs told me. As long as our neighbourhood wasn't dangerous, and it's not, our family would *choose* (knowing we did have the choice) to stay here, keeping our sangfroid and living a life that ran counter to what we'd seen in the No-Go Zone blaring news. And in the end (and this is where it's selfish, she said), our kids wouldn't have to be so frightened as their peers, nor would they necessarily have the same sheltered world view I had. A world of cushiness may await them anyway, so until then they will see what mass migration does to people on both sides, and the real effects of lingering civil war and the ravages of drugs. They'll meet refugee dentists who are living on the sidewalk, and they'll be friends with children whose parents might be deported and who don't have one tenth of what they have, but seem happy and get better grades. That experience can't be quantified, says my smarter wife, and it ingrains in a person a rare quality – something she feels will separate Otto and Bibi from their future peers – of compassion, 'which is a better fuel for life than obscure fear'. Anaïs is always very poetic about these things.

Sure, we could have moved to another neighbourhood in Paris, where streets were cleaner and ruined lives were less in-your-face, but those places were equally upsetting, just in other ways. Instagram-addicted mean girls had bullied Bibi during her first year at the select international school. Other kids were having druggy blow-out parties while their parents were off for the weekend in Deauville. A couple we knew who had a scrumptious apartment in the Seventeenth was living (literally) pay cheque to pay cheque although both had good jobs. And when we did consider other apartments in other neighbourhoods (after I insisted), each place seemed stuck in a time warp or cut off from reality, at least from our reality. Whether it was in the Fourteenth or Fifteenth, even Montmartre, everything seemed so clean and functioning, it almost seemed fake. The gourmet delis and Lacoste boutiques and chicken rotisseries and crayon-coloured vegetable stands all of a sudden seemed rich to me, as in German chocolate cake rich, indigestible, too much. Touristy, even. Something I'd once assumed was the embodiment of French wonderfulness, which now I couldn't stomach.

So, we've stayed.

Minutes after France's victory in the 2018 World Cup, we found ourselves *en famille*, flowing down the bank of the Canal Saint-Martin, caught up in a parallel river of high-fiving revellers and ecstatic fans dancing in the street, waving flags and holding up those in cars who were stupid enough to drive after a World Cup victory.

Soon we were at Place de la République, in the same spot we'd come to years earlier to honour the victims of the terrorist attacks at the Bataclan club and *Charlie Hebdo* offices. But tonight, instead of a solemn candlelit vigil, the place was pandemonium. Some fans had even managed to scale the sixty-foot bronze statue of *République*, clinging to her smaller sisters *Liberté, Egalité, Fraternité*, hanging over each a sign saying '*Cimer Les Bleus*' (the *verlan* version of *Merci Les Bleus*). Caught up in the moment, I mistakenly let Bibi jump on my shoulders, forgetting she was sixteen now. And, while she waved her French flag and her bony hips dug deep into my collarbone, I grinned through the pain, because it seemed like only yesterday she lived on those shoulders, eating her Nutella crêpes while we walked through these same parts, searching for the Place's carousel.

Later that night, we passed by Le Carillon, which resembled more a beach shack at high tide than a Parisian café. The beer on the floor measured almost half an inch, and outside, where just a few years earlier bodies had littered the sidewalk covered in emergency aluminium space blankets, people hugged and sang 'La Marseillaise' and vomited off to the side while still pumping their fists. Joy had reclaimed its place here. The sangfroid was red and pumping.

We then made our way home, limping on sore feet, Otto and Najl-Adams walking ahead of us, wrapped in their French flags, looking like old ladies with shawls. Like many on the national team, both were French kids and sons of immigrants. Both made fun of their fathers' accents, and both had laughed at their dads' respective country's teams that had failed to even qualify for the Cup.

And, as we all sang, a slew of recently penned soccer chants celebrating *Les Bleus* and our Tenth Arrondissement's shining moment, it hit me. What better place could one live in right now? Nothing interesting or original would ever come from my hanging out in the Café Flore or walking the Seine or rewatching *Amélie*, which (and the critics were right) now totally looks dated and clichéd.

Better to be on the front lines in Paris's No-Go Zone, a place where men chased men with bricks, and all you had to do was sit back and watch it from your Berlusconi, knowing nobody in Paris had such a good view.

CHAPTER SIX

HUGE IN FRANCE

I'VE LEARNED THAT, IF YOU LIVE IN FRANCE and you're American, the chances are you didn't come here for the job prospects. It could have been that bar exam you failed, or the year-long sabbatical that became five, but it's rare to find the expat who tells you. 'My career just took off, and they sent me to Paris!' And if by some miracle you are successful here, it has less to do with your talent and more to do with the French not knowing any better. The French, I've found, are a lot more suspicious of other French than they are of Americans. You could be a fugitive sought by Interpol, but if you say you're bilingual and have work experience, they're happy to take your word for it.

At least that's how it has gone for me. When I tell people I live in Paris and write for *Vanity Fair*, they assume I followed the Medill School of Journalism–local paper–assistant editor–editor–contributor trajectory, toiling in the bowels of Condé Nast. It's been everything but that. I took work where I could find it, knowing it would pay off not just immediately in terms of money, but down the line, too, in one form or another, just as long as I jotted it all down in a journal. And working in Paris has another advantage. When my friends in the States ask me what I'm up to nowadays, I'm quick to remind them of lots. 'Even if you haven't heard about me here,' I tell them, 'I'm pretty huge in France.'

Before the magazine work came along, I took just about any job that paid – writing, doing voice-overs, even a spell acting on TV (we'll come to that). I did much of this work for money, of course, because I had mouths to feed, but the immigrant experience somehow lends itself to a *create your own adventure* mentality, giving you the illusion you're fulfilling some sort of passionate bucket-list Hemingway journey when in fact you're translating the Pullman Hotel catalogue.

With its 15 per cent unemployment and measly 1 per cent annual growth, France isn't the place one expects to find immediate work. But that's the beauty of moving to a foreign country. You get to reboot not only your address, but your CV, too. Never once have I been the most qualified or the best suited for a job. But each time I was the most American, and that carried weight. French companies often like to think of themselves or their product as global, and the chance to work with a real, live, flesh-and-blood American is one that's just too good to pass up.

What's not really known outside of France is that the wine industry isn't doing so well. You can go online and buy a vineyard and château for a song. They're so cheap, they've become the new yacht, meaning they're affordable at the beginning but ruinously expensive to maintain, and are usually purchased by Russians. Somebody told me once,

'John, if you want to buy a vineyard, you better have the money to buy five vineyards.'

Bordeaux and Burgundy wines no longer have the cachet they used to and, because of that, the company that contacted me, OVS (Opéra Vins et Spiritueux), was looking to copy the success of the Australians, of all people. Their goal was to make the ultimate oxymoron, a French Yellow Tail, which they called *Chamarré* ('richly brocaded', if that means anything to you) and their business plan of throwing together *vin de pays* (wine produced from a variety of different vineyards), slapping an animal on the label, and figuring out a catchy slogan to sell it by the caseload at American point-of-purchase displays was so cynical, it couldn't possibly fail.

OVS was the first French wine company to be floated on the French stock exchange. They'd raised more than €7.2 million in capital, but the fact they were coming to me, someone with no real experience either in advertising or in wine, should have indicated that they had fundamental problems. Sure, it's not unheard of for outsiders to offer 'a new set of eyes' for a campaign or a marketing launch or an event. But to OVS, my American eye was more important than my 'book' (something advertising people have and I didn't), and when I simply said *Je m'appelle John'* with my American accent at our introductory meeting, it was clear from their faces that they thought I was the man for the job.

At first, I assumed OVS wanted me to help create a new name for their wine, only because the one they had, *Chamarré*, sucked so bad. To me it was a name created in a Eurotrash lab. It couldn't have been more obnoxious if it tried. Just pronouncing it sounded like a pretentious American trying to sound French; the kind I see on occasion in boulangeries who go out of their way to say *croissant* as *krois-sans*, without the *t*, or who refuse to pronounce *Cannes* like *Anne* with a C (the correct way) and instead blurt out *Kahn*, as in *Wrath of* (the wrong way).

I had done my research and compiled a list of other wines in the *Chamarré* range that had found success with distinctive names that had humour built in: Fat Bastard, Red Truck, Goats do Roam, all of them brilliant. For that reason, I felt OVS's wine had to go the self-mocking route, because, in my non-advertising, non-wine, non-industry experience opinion, it would be really funny for a French company to hark back to its heritage while poking fun at itself. I even thought of going all the way and calling it French Snob. 'Because, let's be honest,' I told them at our introductory meeting, 'how awesome would it be for a dinner conversation to start with *This French Snob tastes delish.*'

Unfortunately, the room didn't feel the same. For them, *Chamarré* had that (and I love using this expression because Americans say it more than the French) *je ne sais quoi*. It sounded French, refined and super-forgetful. And it had a multicoloured butterfly (recalling Yellow Tail's kangaroo) on the label. 'John, you're American,' said one of the marketers at our second meeting. 'How do you think we can launch this butterfly and gain ground on American market share, so that *Chamarré* can battle Yellow Tail, Red Truck and Fat Bastard?' He said this with a French accent so that *Bastard* sounded like '*BasTARD*,' which made me squeal with delight only because it felt as if I was in an *Austin Powers* scene and the enemies had just been named.

'Well,' I said in the Don Draper voice I brought for the occasion, 'from my experience' (which almost made me laugh), and then I shared with them the epiphany I'd written the week earlier. 'You have to give them a Coke/Pepsi choice. And for me that would be the following – *Don't be a wino, be a why yes. Drink Chamarré.*' The phrase brought everything together in one fluid stroke. It would not only be a call to arms for drinking responsibly (Americans love that shit even though they never follow it), it could be the Grey Poupon mustard line for millennials. Instead of the infamous 'but of course' sendoff, *Chamarré* ads would feature a man offering a woman a glass in some fancy hotel, always with the catch line '*Chamarré*, Madame?' To which she'd respond, 'Why yes.'

I finished the presentation expecting applause but found a stern-looking crowd of French people exchanging confused looks. I knew I'd flopped when the first question posed was: 'Wait. What's a wino?' My wino/why yes campaign was DOA. I was paid for my time, and the company decided to go with some watered-down time-honoured faux-creative idea centred on 'The Butterfly Effect' – that notion that a small action ripples out to create bigger, more dramatic outcomes because, of course, drinking a gulp of *Chamarré* could be a catalyst for world peace.

I won't go into more detail about the campaign. It's just too sad. But what my *Chamarré* experience encapsulated was watching a disruptive idea get watered down before it had even passed Go. In OVS's case, they were brazen enough to hire an American to adapt an American campaign based on what he thought would be American funny, only to settle on an approach they were more familiar with. Time after time, a lot of the French I've come across want to channel an American style of hip, but can't begin to grasp just how depraved and horrible we actually are.

OVS eventually filed for bankruptcy and was liquidated. And no, not one American has ever heard of *Chamarré*. Anaïs, however, still has a pair of those American Apparel short shorts I made for the presentation, which I explained could be shamelessly sold in tandem with multiple cases of *Chamarré*. And when I see her walking in them with a *why yes* and a *wino* on each cheek, I'm reminded of what gloriously could have been.

During my first few years here, I watched a lot of French TV. I told Anaïs it was a way for me to improve my comprehension, but in reality I had a morbid fascination with the whole thing. I was tantalised by reality shows that showed people actually fucking in Jacuzzis and by French talk shows that weren't scripted and might end with the guest telling the host to 'get a real job'. Presidential debates had the candidates facing each other but seated like opposing counsels in a conference room. All the weathermen were weatherwomen, and each was cast the same way: svelte, in a skirt and high heels, and always more than fifty-eight years old. There were awards shows that were poorly scripted and never predictable. A drunken Gérard Depardieu assured us of that. And then there were the American reruns, fifteen years late, which allowed you to catch up on series like *MacGyver* or *Charmed* and remind yourself why you didn't watch them in the first place.

At its core, there's a pejorative line of thinking that festers inside French TV. It's that the audience, for whatever reason, is moronic. French TV never had its *Honeymooners*, *M*A*S*H*, *Seinfeld* heyday. Its writers never came from the *Harvard Lampoon*. TV was for *les masses*, and it was the French producer who knew better than the audience what we would like. TV is used to move soap, I was told. And, because of this approach, there's not the same quality control.

I'd love to tell you my sheer comedic talent got me hired as an actor for an *SNL*-type show, but in reality it was (again) because I was American. The premise and format of the show was not unlike Garry Shandling's *The Larry Sanders Show* or *30 Rock,* a show within a show. A fairly well-known actress in real life (we'll call her Aurélie) was getting her own series on Canal+ (the HBO of France). My fictional character was to be her manager/agent, guiding her through the intricacies of TV production, advising her based on all my experience back in the States. To the French, I was Ari Gold from *Entourage* but not so sleazy (I think).

Oh, I should also probably mention that I'd never acted in my life. But that was okay, apparently. Just as with advertising, the only thing that mattered was that I was American and spoke French with an accent. And no, Anaïs wasn't jealous. French TV has such a bad reputation with her crowd, a role on a comedy show is looked upon like a gig on Home Shopping Network. When the producers told me I'd been hired, I was so excited, I doubled down and told them, 'Look, if you really want it to be American, you better have an American writing for you guys, as well.' They were intrigued, I could tell, and when they asked if I'd written for TV before, my response was (because I was holding the same spiral notebook I used for the *Chamarré* campaign), 'Why yes.'

My Ari Gold role as Aurélie's producer/agent was scrapped after the pilot. They found it/me too negative and difficult to understand. 'Who is he again? Her gay friend? Why is he angry all the time?' Luckily, though, I'd managed to weasel my way into a desk on the set, and so my role morphed into journalist. The idea this time was that I'd report the nightly news like *SNL*'s 'Weekend Update', but since my character was American, I wouldn't have much command of the French language, so would have to act out the news. For example, if there was violence in the Middle East, instead of describing which factions were fighting, I'd simulate a machine gun firing and jump around on one leg. I'd also scream a lot. They wanted lots of screaming. Since the other writers had seen Fox News a couple of times, they assumed that's how Americans reported the news. And they weren't completely wrong.

As a writer, I was tasked with delivering a series of sketches each week. Since they were in French, I was more worried that the show runners would notice my grammatical errors than whether my jokes or sketches landed comically. I even went so far as to hire, with my own money, a translator to make sure each page was perfect. But this proved more difficult than I thought, seeing as she often didn't understand the context of the jokes.

On Monday morning, I'd arrive at our writer meeting with a stapled version of each episode in duplicates of six for everyone to read. I also brought coffee. I'd dreamed of having a TV writing job since I was kid, only because, just once, I wanted to sit around an oval table and 'punch up' scripts and throw pencils at the wall and have Harvard guys make my *Simpsons* draft better. It was like the coronation of being funny. Unfortunately, I found myself often alone on these Monday mornings. The rest of the writers would show up late, having been out partying the night before, and they would eventually arrive hideously hungover. The first hour was spent on '*le débrief*', with everyone discussing what had gone down at the Costes Hotel bar. I'd sit and smile through the pain of not having been invited to the party, looking at my pile of scripts sitting there waiting to be read.

When the show runner finished his monologue about being hammered with a semi-celebrity and how she was obviously cheating on her star boyfriend, he'd glance through some of my sketches with a straight face, then look up at the others as if something I'd written had triggered an idea. 'He liked something!' I'd tell myself. 'Maybe we could oval table this?' 'What are we ordering for lunch?' he'd say, putting my scripts to the side. Soon everyone had left the room. My pile of scripts would sit there the entire week, and, as the weeks grew, so would the pile. Higher and higher it would rise, unread and unopened.

Since the show was a weekly, the writers were asked to write over the weekend, then polish the scripts Monday and Tuesday. We'd shoot the show Wednesday, which was then edited Thursday and Friday for a Sunday-night broadcast. In reality, the scripts (that were used) were written by three guys (not me) on Tuesday afternoon after their fifth joint and, at 5pm, the final drafts were printed and sent to the actors two floors down in the studio to rehearse.

When I say 'three guys' I mean the head writer, his best friend, and a guy who typed while they kicked a soccer ball back and forth. The rest of us sat on the couch and contributed laughter and smiles when needed. Since I was being paid a lot, nobody wanted to hear me complain.

The worst part of this experience was that I was an actor as well, so I'd watch, in real time, the scenes that had been written for me unfold, each one more humiliating than the next. 'Let's have John be Spider-Man,' said one writer, high as shit, with me sitting next to him, but as if I wasn't in the room. 'And' (he'd take a longer hit on his joint) 'Spider-Man doesn't want to work in France or doesn't get the French.' He'd then start laughing hysterically at this premise and I'd nervously laugh with him. We all would. '*Oui,*' the head writer would jump in. 'And he descends from a string into the office each morning and fucks everything up!' (another long toke). 'Because he doesn't want to work here!' 'Ha, yeah!!' The room would erupt.

The next day, not only was I dressed up in a fake muscled Spider-Man outfit, but I had French lines to memorise in a few hours. And I was hanging by a cable upside down, because 'Spider-Man doesn't just enter by the door, John.'

This was a year of my life. Ironically, my Spider-Man episode turned out to be the highlight of the season. In the months that followed, as the ratings dropped, I'd find myself on the bad side of Aurélie, who felt my 'Weekend Update' was stealing her thunder. Since my sketches were not read, the executive producers assumed I was lazy. Aurélie, feeling the scripts were not up to snuff, brought in another band of writers she trusted. The staff writers, the ones who didn't write until Tuesday afternoon, said she wasn't being professional and began writing bad lines for her on purpose. (At least I hope they were on purpose.) Soon, nobody was talking, the environment was toxic, and the press was savage. The worst article carried a cover headline 'Is This a Joke?' beside a photo of me as Spider-Man, smiling like an idiot.

Following Christmas break, the network decided our show would not be renewed, which is normal for TV. What was bizarre was that they wanted us to complete the season, right up until June. Six long months ensued and, since everyone wanted to protect their careers, John assumed the majority of the sketches: I was a Belgian secret agent, a coked-up producer at the Cannes Film Festival, a radical far-right protester who bullied bearded Muslims ...

Even Otto and Bibi, who were two and six at the time, could see the show sucked. The excitement of watching their father on TV waned with each passing week. Now, all they said as we watched the episode together on Sunday night was 'Dad, you screamed a lot,' or 'Dad, is that actress being mean to you?' Following the last taping, there was a wrap party, and one of the writers had the chutzpah to claim, 'We were ahead of our time. France wasn't ready for a show like this.' I smiled and agreed and asked him if I could have my scripts back. I also asked for the Spider-Man outfit, which I kept for Halloween.

Following my brief stint on TV, I wanted out of show business and back into the friendly confines of magazine writing. 'Paris's Top Ten Vegan Restaurants' and 'Shoes to Wear at a Summer Wedding' articles no longer seemed painful compared to the humiliation I'd just experienced. What I learned, though, was that you can't run from your past. Soon enough, I was being offered lucrative side work doing voice-overs in English.

Doing English voice-over work in France is probably no different from doing voice-overs in the US, except that there are fewer Anglophone actors to compete with here in France. Often, I was providing an English voice for a French commercial that was trying to win an award at Cannes or making what the industry calls a *maquette* (mock-up), which is a film the ad agency pitches to their client to convince them to invest in the real film with better music, 3D effects and, of course, a better voice actor.

I also dubbed a lot of documentaries for the American or British TV market or, on rare occasions, dubbed a French film into English. What always struck me as comical was that budgets for these things aren't small. The director, the actors and the post-production all cost a lot, and yet much of the product's success rested on a guy whose voice was chosen because he played Spider-Man on an unwatched series.

One time, I was asked to do a commercial for Gillette. The director met with me and another actor before the recording and showed us the film, describing its tone as 'skate and thrash meets Beastie Boys.' (Since he was French, he pronounced *thrash* as *trash* and *Boys* without the *s*, so it sounded funnier.) Gillette was moving into the youth market, he said, and targeting consumers who were buying their first razors. That's why they were going with snowboarders and skaters and why the script's dialogue featured lines like:

'Are you looking for a thrashing shave?'

'Word!'

'The Gillette so and so rocks the burn and the chaff with a two-sided system that'll not only blow your mind but give you that ultimate swag.'

'Word!'

During the take, while half-pipes and skate parks jumped off the screen, I rattled off the lines as best I could, 'Cutting action whose razor edge or something or other won't let you down,' in what I thought to be a Southern California surfer's voice. I was excited to try a new accent. Too often I'm asked to produce what the French call 'the mid-Atlantic', an accent European clients say is in between British and American, something refined yet approachable, something you might think Julia Child or William F. Buckley used to speak. The French love the mid-Atlantic accent, but they have no idea what it really sounds like.

During our recording, I noticed my co-actor was having trouble with our back and forth. He couldn't find a proper rhythm. His English was fine, but it was as if he'd never been in a situation like this before. He wasn't jumping on the phrases like you should, or zinging me back with a convincing high five of 'Dude, totally!' Something smelled foreign to me, and after three takes I realised what it was. He was Australian, and struggling with the mid-Atlantic.

The studio had given him the lion's share of the dialogue. The man was labouring. 'It's Wahn ryezah for whan killah shayve.' I assumed, of course, the production company knew all this. They wouldn't have hired an Australian not knowing the lead voice wasn't American, would they? So I spoke up.

'Should we switch and maybe I could try Mark's role, just because I'm not sure it works with his Australian accent.'

'Who's Australian?' the recording studio voice came through our headsets.

I pointed to Mark like a child would a classmate who'd convinced him to shoplift. Mark stared back at me, his eyes pleading for me to shut up, and I knew I'd blown it.

'Mark, is this true?' said a scolding voice.

'Yes,' Mark sighed, 'I'm Australian.' He looked at me in squinted defeat as if to say *I hope you're happy!*

I wanted to die. I'd committed the unpardonable offence of voice-over etiquette, an etiquette I would have known to follow had I done more voice-overs.

'Let's take five,' the voice in the headsets said, leaving Mark and me alone in an airless booth, both staring at the floor. Our phones were in our coats on the other side of the glass, so we couldn't look at them to avoid each other's eyes.

'Sorry, dude,' I turned to him, still using my skater accent. 'I didn't know. I mean, I thought they knew, you know?'

'No worries, mate,' Mark said. 'You're a cunt.'

The voice on the headphones came back within minutes. 'I think there's been a mix-up, guys, and Mark, sorry, but we need to change voices. Now, John? Just so we're clear. Are you American?'

'Yes. I. Am,' I said proudly, waving to Mark as he left the booth. I'd already forgotten what had transpired and turned back to the client. 'Do you need me to do both versions now?'

Once I was asked to dub John McEnroe's voice for the car manufacturer Seat. In the film, McEnroe had parked his car illegally. And, since he didn't have a Seat (a smaller car), his vehicle stretched beyond the marked lines, and a cop was issuing him a ticket. Of course, and in classic McEnroe fashion, the tennis star argued with the police officer, shouting at him, 'But it's on the line! Look! It's on the line!'

The film, I admit, was pretty funny, but the production company didn't want McEnroe's lines in English. They wanted him to speak French with a classic twangy American accent. So, for close to an hour, I watched the prompter and repeated the same line in poorly pronounced French, trying to match John McEnroe's enraged lips as much as possible. '*C'était sur la ligne!! Regardez! C'est sur la ligne!!*'

After twenty takes, I could tell the client still wasn't happy, so I offered up an idea. 'Perhaps it would be better if you just kept the English version and subtitled it. It might even be funnier to watch McEnroe interact with the policeman.'

There was silence in the booth. Then one of the producers said, '*C'est pas con*' ('That's not completely stupid'), which I took as a compliment. French has become so sarcastic and negative that 'not insanely moronic' is actually more positive than *c'est vraiment du génie!* (that's genius), which, of course, means the opposite, that you're a total idiot.

Anaïs also does voice-overs, and one time we were hired as a duo to translate and dub into French a series of *For*

Dummies films, namely *Pilates for Dummies* and *Yoga for Dummies*. The plan was that I'd first translate the English into French, then Anaïs would translate my French into real French. Afterwards, Anaïs would record the scripts in a studio. The producer hired us because we were cheaper than the competition (professionals who knew how much to properly bid). Plus, he felt a husband-and-wife team would work well together, which let me know loud and clear that this man had never been married.

We fought horribly throughout the production process. Anaïs is a perfectionist, and she insisted on finding the exact translation for every phrase. For example, with 'build the core', she smelled a rat when I tried to sneak in a literal translation, '*Construisez le core.*'

'But that doesn't mean anything!' she yelled, ordering me to fetch the Collins Robert dictionary.

'But it doesn't mean anything in English, either!' I yelled back. 'And why do we have to be so thorough, anyway,' I'd scream. 'It's fucking *Pilates for Dummies!*'

But she was right. A job is a job. And I reminded her of that when she had to record the French voice-over, her enthusiasm waning each time she was forced to mimic a peppy American woman in Spandex shouting into the microphone, 'Are you ready to work those rock-hard abs?'

'Yes we are!' I'd yell to Anaïs behind the glass.

Another time, a producer who'd read some of my magazine pieces contacted me with an idea. He wanted to create an animation series based on talking sausages. Yup, sausages that talk. And, since sausages differ in length and colour and texture, he told me, we already had a varied cast. The idea was to film a bunch of them on a green screen, superimpose just the actors' lips onto the sausages, insert a background like a high school gym or office and let the hijinks ensue. The idea seemed easy enough. Comedy Central had even done something similar with sock puppets, so *pourquoi pas?*

The problem, this time, was me. I tried to be too clever. The producers wanted typecast characters for a dumbed-down audience, meaning the merguez sausage might be Arabic and speak in Parisian slang. The frankfurter might have a German accent and wear Lederhosen, and the kielbasa would be Polish and a plumber.

Instead, I treated the sausages as if they were real people with complex lives. One was an Ikea bed salesman who laced his sales pitches with crude sexual innuendo. There was a sausage named Dan, who always had to tell you that the party you were both at was awesome. There was a sausage who speed dated but was paranoid the person across from him had been sent by his ex.

Like the *Chamarré* people, the producers wanted an American to write the series, just not this American. The pilot was never picked up. However, five years later, in the metro, I noticed a poster for a movie called *Sausage Party* produced by the actor Seth Rogen. Had Seth seen my pilot? Probably not. And I'd have to let this all roll off my back, despite the stream of congratulatory emails I received, now that 'my sausage project' had finally gotten picked up.

Little did I know, however, that metro poster fame would shine on me one year later, when, along the walls of most stations in Paris, a life-sized von Sothen began smiling back at everyone. No, it wasn't me. Nor was it Anaïs or the kids. It was my dog, Bogart, who'd been cast in a summer comedy called *Yves*. With a name like Bogart, friends told me I shouldn't have been surprised he was in a movie, but still, without any acting experience or time spent at the Conservatory, Bogart had defied the odds and caught the eye of a casting director out on one of our walks. His first job was for Marks & Spencer, where he posed with reindeer antlers for a Christmas campaign. And, on the heels of that campaign's success, Bogart 'met' with the producer and director of *Yves*, who liked him so much they even wrote additional scenes for him.

To be honest, *Yves* isn't that great. I mean, any film that centres on a down-and-out rapper whose futuristic refrigerator helps turn around his career, isn't long for the box office. But I didn't care. Bogart rocked, and I received cheques for his work, which made me even contemplate setting up a separate bank account, because, you know, royalties and all.

I think what touched me the most seeing Bogart in magazine kiosks and at bus stops and on the big screen throughout the entire summer of 2019, with that jolly open-mouthed mutt smile of his, wasn't just the revenge he was exacting on all of those who'd made fun of his master these past years. Bogart's story kind of mimicked mine. Granted our backgrounds were a bit different. I wasn't found in the street as a baby, then taken to a shelter to be handed to the first family who claimed me. Nor had I been castrated at six months. Yet, like Bogart, I'd found work in this town despite my lack of experience and my inability to speak. And we'd both worked with directors who wrote us into ridiculous situations and put us in comedic positions just because they know we were happy to please and wanted to be loved.

Now Bogart's scheduled to shoot a pilot for a TV series in Belgium, and I sense already by his demeanour that the power dynamic has changed. This time, he – no we – are going to be just a tad more demanding on set.

CHAPTER SEVEN

VOULEZ-VOUS THINK TANK *AVEC MOI?*

WHEN MY PARENTS AND I TOOK our first family trip to Europe, we visited Paris and Amsterdam, Rome and Venice, and in the manner most Americans do – meaning over the course of ten days. At the time, I thought it was normal to run in and out of the Louvre drive-by photographing the *Mona Lisa,* then dashing through the Tuileries Gardens to grab a seat on a *bateau-mouche* to be whisked past the Eiffel Tower so we could catch the overnight train leaving for Marseilles that evening.

Like any nine-year-old travelling American, I was hard to please. Going to Europe hadn't been my idea and, although I went through the motions and aped interest, my mind was focused more on playing Galaga and Pac-Man inside random cafés than sitting outside *en terrasse* with my parents. I preferred feeding the pigeons at Piazza San Marco to actually visiting the Piazza San Marco.

But the one time I was floored and shaken to my core by Europe was when we visited Cassis, a charming seaside town near Marseilles. Cassis is the kind of place you've seen reproduced in Matisse paintings: charming white and turquoise boats bouncing in the harbour, older men playing *boules* in low-cut Speedos, café regulars sprawled over chairs with their shirts opened, chests tanned and gold chains sparkling in the sun, while the pastis flows like a ruptured water main.

I'd been watching this scene from my perch next to the beach's public changing booths, waiting for my parents to arrive, wondering if by any chance there might be a sit-down Space Invaders in one of the cafés. Just then, an adult brunette waltzed by wearing sunglasses and a headscarf, bikini bottoms and no top. Before my mouth could register a gawk, I found myself at arm's length from two exposed breasts. The woman was on her way to the bathroom. She shut the door behind her, leaving me dumbfounded. For me, it was like spotting a giant squid, something that in nature humans rarely get to see, and yet here I was watching it live. And what was nuts was that to leave the restroom this woman was going to reappear, likely still topless.

By then, my parents had also surfaced, holding towels and a picnic, bitching as they had the whole trip that we didn't have much time to lose if we wanted to visit the Château d'If prison and the Vieux-Port de Marseille and see where Gene Hackman filmed *The French Connection*. I limped along reluctantly, knowing nobody at home would believe my story; why hadn't I thought to take a photo? It wasn't until I tossed my towel down and looked toward the waves that I realised the woman in the bathroom was not an outlier. A sea of humanity was lying down or standing up right next to me, all of them topless.

Suddenly everything went silent for me. A Steadicam zoom-in of my face would have revealed a stunned-looking boy staring straight ahead at the water as if he'd witnessed a shark attack. I was both scared and embarrassed, not just because everyone was naked, but because I worried that they might notice me staring. Plus, I had my parents to consider. Neither had had anything to do with the sexual revolution. They'd grown up in the prim 1950s and listened to Count Basie. My mother had gone to Vassar and called dog shit 'dog dirt', and when she drank too much at a party, she'd claim the next day she'd been 'overserved'. They weren't prudes, but they definitely weren't *libertines*, either, and when they were in my presence anything sexual on screen or in real life only caused fussing and fidgeting.

I jumped into the water to collect my bearings, sinking to eye-level depth where I could subtly look back at the sand and all of the topless women on it. There in the cool Mediterranean Sea, the unthinkable soon became banal, the *exotique* eventually *quotidien*. Within a half-hour I was strolling down the beach in my Ferrari fold-up glasses, watching half-naked women of all ages promenade past me, smiling stupidly at my dumb fucking luck.

It was during this stroll, with Rod Stewart crackling inside some beachside café nearby, that the purpose of France hit me: you could actually live like this. It was legal. And, for a nine-year-old, the realisation wasn't framed in a repressed or unchained context, or as Latin versus Puritan, but just as a rock-and-roll celebration of life, one expressed through sex.

The boy came home changed that summer. My trip to France gave me the impression I was more sexually advanced than my peers. When they riffled through *Playboy* magazine and showed me centrefolds up in their attic, I'd shrug with blasé disdain as if to say, 'Whatever'. Sex didn't need to be snuck around on or leered at in private. It was out there for everyone to see on a tiny beach in a country far across the sea. And one day, I promised them and myself, I'd live there and prosper and have all the sex I wanted.

♙ ♙ ♙

When I returned to France as an adult, I was immediately disappointed that it wasn't as I'd so vividly remembered: It was grey and cramped and the people weren't as topless as I wanted them to be. I was only at the baggage claim of Charles de Gaulle Airport, but still.

Ever since that fateful trip to Cassis, I'd been building France up in my head as a hedonistic land of transgression, mythologising French women to the point of fetishism. Unlike my friends who dreamed about Michelle Pfeiffer or Kim Basinger or Farrah Fawcett, I was more into French actresses such as Anne Parillaud, who'd starred in the 1980s Luc Besson thriller *La Femme Nikita* or Béatrice Dalle from the bleak *Betty Blue*, films I'd seen on video or in French class. In fact, the only American actress I did find sexy was Nastassja Kinski, but she wasn't even American, was she?

During college and afterward, I found myself dating French women, but at the time I was never allowed to call it a date, at least not to their faces. For them, the entire institution of 'dating' was fraudulent. They were fine with getting a drink with you, but under one condition: nothing could be formally organised. They wanted spontaneity, as if we both had stumbled on the same sushi restaurant in the East Village at the same time and, since we were both there, well, we might as well share a table, right?

They also didn't want a lot of questions thrown their way. Asking them where they were from or what they did for a living wasn't showing interest. It was conducting an interview. And there was nothing more wet-blankety and romance-killing for a French woman than to be asked on a date, and asked questions on that date.

Whereas they'd insist on ambiguity during the meet-and-greet process, they were brutally upfront as to what would happen later on sexually if they found you appealing. These French women didn't mess around. All of the jumping through hoops (the first date, the dinner, then the invite over to meet friends, then the weekend together) American women pulled, French women found childish and a waste of time. For them, sleeping with the person wasn't the big deal; it was poetic and impromptu. And once a French woman decided to go there with you, she was all in, which sometimes meant doing it on the first date (which you weren't allowed to call a date). Afterward, though, she was your woman and you were her man, and it wasn't pushy for her to make plans to move in. Her approach to dating was a mix of sexual liberty and old-country tradition. The act of sleeping with someone was taken super-seriously, and they weren't buying the convenient out that I and many of my American friends (men and women both) had perfected of 'wanting to keep our space' or 'take things slow'.

🏠 🏠 🏠

All of this may sound tame in the age of Tinder, but for me the French woman's approach to sex was pretty out there. And now that I was living in the country where these women were made, the stuff I saw on a daily basis only confirmed my preconceptions. On TV, there were French commercials flashing nudity to sell shower gels. The equivalents of *US*

Weekly featured celebs, not topless, but bottomless, and Paris pharmacies sold cellulite cream the old-fashioned way, by placing a giant poster of an arched back and a woman's ass with a thong in the window. My dreary airport arrival had been the exception, I realised, and as I passed a club in the Quartier Pigalle named Sexodrome, my preconceptions were confirmed.

I once saw a jewellery ad on the metro going for the hard sell without irony: 'Give your mistress something special for the holidays.' A recent ad for condoms showed a hotel room and the tag line below it read, 'Sarah and Jonathan shared one in room #436.'

As the years passed, I'd grow accustomed to this live-and-let-live approach to sex and discarded whatever shred of American Puritanism had made the journey to France with me. Even if a situation or person wasn't sexualised, I'd find some way to put sex on the table. 'Those neighbours are total swingers,' I'd tell myself in the kitchen. 'Just look at the way they stared at us at dinner. Typical.' 'Did that mother just hit on me at school? Of course she did. They do that kind of thing here.'

I read propositions into every encounter – at the gym, at parties, at the office – and sometimes my impression was confirmed. The man at the dog park actually *did* ask if I wanted to catch a sauna with him. The woman at the... nope, the man at the dog park was the only one.

But it wasn't all in my head.

Échangisme, the French term for spouse swapping, had become the *'it'* (the French pronounce it 'heat' and each time I'm thrown) topic of French society in the 2000s. There were tell-all books by former *échangistes* and bestselling books centring on *échangisme*. And there was a popular TV show called *Paris Dernier*. The host would visit Paris's hippest bars and discotheques every Saturday night, interviewing tipsy stars and starlets, usually with a handheld camera, getting them to say stuff they'd regret the next day. The show would routinely end with the host stumbling into a '*club échangiste*' at 3am, camera at the ready, where he'd interview guests and then film them screwing. It was a smash hit. To many Parisians, *Paris Dernier* was the French *SNL*. To me, it was quite possibly TV's finest moment.

The *échangisme* craze fed off a mix of paranoia and imagination. Your neighbour, your friends, your dentist – anybody could be an *échangiste*. You just had to be clever enough to read the signs. During my first few years in France, every dinner party was like a game of Russian roulette, with couples wondering if other couples were going to pop the question over dinner.

Of course, during all of this craziness, I was happily married to a wife I adored, but whose position on *échangisme* has never been made clear. For all I knew, Anaïs was a legendary *échangiste*, too, and was simply waiting for me to give the green light. Yet, on the other hand, if she wasn't, I didn't want to be the first to say, 'Honey, so what do you think about all this swapping business anyway?' She'd only interpret that as my wanting to try, and then I'd be in the *merde*. Because the sad truth was that, deep down, Mr Topless-Beach-Wants-to-Move-to-France-for-all-the-Sex-He-Can-Eat doesn't have the guts to try anything.

Around this time, I was approached by a friend of Anaïs's called Jeanne to join what I guess you could call a 'salon'. Some might call it a reflection group, others a lodge, and if you really want to sound pretentious, you could probably call it a think tank. Regardless of the name, the idea of joining something, anything, like this intrigued me. It seemed Parisian and literary and refined, so as an American living here you can imagine how flattered I was.

The past few years in Paris had not always lived up to my expectations. The Hemingway lifestyle I'd envisioned for myself – café hopping and writing in parks – had crashed on the rocks of my present reality: pushing a stroller and drawing in a sandpit with Bibi. Here, I thought, was a chance to finally fill out the image I'd had of myself *before* I arrived: as a sort of Noël Coward/Dick Cavett type, holding court over a reading of Sartre. I would treat this not just as an invitation, but as recognition, for all the hard work I'd put in to becoming a *real* expat – and another in a long line of benchmarks I'd meet on the road to becoming fully French. I'd also done the math at home and realised Bibi, who was six, had more friends than I did, which obviously sparked some jealousy. If nothing else, joining this group would help even the score.

But a club? I'd never been part of a club before. Teams, sure, baseball, football, basketball, but clubs? They were for nerds, *non*? When I was a student, the more clubs you were in, the fewer friends you had. But the name of this group had flair: *Futurbulence*. Just by the title you could tell it had its focus on a turbulent future. My kind of group. Much jazzier than its passive American counterparts Aspen or Mensa, which I imagined were peopled by guys wearing light blue oxfords and khakis in a 'dress-down Friday' way, their cellphones clipped to their belts.

Now, the way the selection of a *Futurbulent* works is that they interview you – twice. Why two times, I don't know. The first interview was conducted in machine-gun French by two women over lunch, and I left feeling unsure I'd even sat at the right table. Quick talkers and quick thinkers, these two waxed on about sustainable development and micro-loans and the Marshall Fund and we hadn't even ordered yet.

I smiled and let them go on, all the while holding myself back from interrupting midstream to admit that I really wasn't smart. But it didn't matter, it seemed. I wasn't being judged on my merits, but on my pedigree – the rationale being, if their group was to resemble anything futuristic and turbulent, they'd better have an American on board *tout de suite*. Over the entrée, the conversation veered toward the mission of *Futurbulence* and the way in which the salon would run. I perked up and held on as best I could.

'There'll be long dinners, of course,' they explained, 'and role-playing.'

Silence on my end.

'Themes will be chosen. We'll often break off into groups, and special guests sometimes are invited.'

More silence.

Long alcohol-fuelled dinners, breaking off into groups, role-playing, and guests invited on occasion. All they'd left out, it seemed, were the pig masks. Was all of this a pretext for sex? Was this a salon for *échangistes* and thus something I should avoid? But my curiosity got the best of me.

The more I imagined this group as a sex club, the more I feared being rejected. It's humiliating to know people don't find you attractive. And, as the days passed, I slipped into a micro-depression, thinking not that I hadn't impressed them with my intellect or pedigree, but that I wasn't hot enough.

Then I got the second call, this time from someone named Stanislas. He and another member would meet me for the second interview . . . this time for drinks. Apparently in

Futurbulence, the girls do lunch – the guys do drinks. So, we shared beers, and they also spoke fast, but this time, it wasn't about role-playing or pairing off. It was about keeping this all a secret. As in, 'Are we safe, John?'

Later that month I received an email telling me I'd been accepted, but the elation quickly fizzled into apprehension. It's one thing to yearn to be part of the group, it's another thing to cavalierly accept their invitation to join. What the hell had I gotten into?

Another email soon arrived, this one a mass message to all the other *Futurbulents* 'Re: the welcoming of our new member – John von Sothen, at our usual spot – the Red Throat.' The Red Throat? I mean, really. And where is this located?

I grew nauseated and quickly confided my dilemma and fear to Anaïs, only for her to laugh in my face and recount it to our friends over dinner the next night. 'John thinks he's been invited to an *échangiste* club,' she announced. I quickly left the table to fetch dessert.

'An *échangiste* club? But you're not going to let him go, are you?' asked an astonished friend.

'Of course, it's not that.' I heard her laugh. 'But you see, he needs to believe these things. If I say anything to the contrary, it would be like telling him there's no Père Noël.'

After our guests left, I told her to stop kidding around, because this time it was serious.

'Well, just don't go,' she countered as she continued to fill the dishwasher. 'Email them and tell them thanks, but no thanks and *basta* ... Can you fill up the coffeemaker for tomorrow?'

'But you know how these people operate.'

She stopped and gave me a long look. 'If they were a real sex club, why would they want you?'

I tried to ignore the personal attack. 'I think it's because I'm American.'

She burst out with a bigger laugh, and I ignored that as well, and went on to explain the international aspect of the group and wonder aloud if they perhaps found me funny. But she was already onto her second question:

'Then why did Jeanne – our friend – think of you?'

I watched as her mind turned and her anger grew. It was the same anger a mother shows when her child shoplifts for the first time. At first, the rage is directed towards the child. But then the mother realises the child's just pathetic and, worse, he's been taken advantage of by even more pathetic peers who talked him into stealing. Therein lies the real blame.

This *Futurbulence* thing isn't the first instance where Anaïs has been forced to bail me out. If she's not having to explain that we *don't* need to buy five calendars from the garbage man each year ('But what if they stop picking up our garbage?' I ask her), she's on the phone with France Telecom pleading that her husband didn't quite understand which soccer subscription he ordered.

Countless times, she's been forced to drag me around the neighbourhood scolding various shopkeepers for ripping me off. All of whom shrug their shoulders as if to say they didn't know I was incompetent.

To the fish guy: 'Does he look like he could eat a kilo of clams?'

'But, Madame...'

To the dry cleaner: 'Do you really think he's someone who wants his jeans pressed?'

'But, Madame...'

And as the door slams, she leads me back down the block. I'd probably suck my thumb if I wasn't holding all the bags of returnables.

Now at the dishwasher, post-dinner, Anaïs was telling me, plain and simple, to hand her the *Futurbulence* phone number, and she would deal with it, as she'd done every other time.

'I don't have their number. They're secret.' All of sudden, I'd become the kid who didn't want his mom to get involved.

The next day I was sent off with strict instructions, so strict it was as if she'd safety-pinned a letter to my chest. I drilled myself on the metro ride there.

'Don't make eye contact; just pay your respects and acknowledge there's been a big misunderstanding. Say you're flattered – start with the ..."Oh, you didn't get my email?" thing.'

I was so busy rehearsing, I didn't realise I'd walked into the Red Throat, and there at the bar stood an older, wiry type, maybe the restaurant owner, maybe the founder, maybe the 'guest of honour'?

'I'm here for *Futurbulence*,' I said meekly, realising how weird that sounded.

'Ah, *Futurbulence*.' He smiled. 'They're in the *back room*.'

Of course they were in the back room. I gulped and shuffled toward a curtain separating *Futurbulence* from decent society. My moral compass would never be true again, and all because I wanted to see for myself the sort of sexual world I thought I'd caught a glimpse of on that Cassis beach.

I took a deep breath and pulled back the curtain, at which point a strange thing happened. There were no capes, no masks. Classic chino khakis, sure, and oxford shirts, check, bottled water, yes, but wine, too, and even champagne.

I shook hands and said my hellos, and everyone was gracious and modest. Some worked in banking, others worked in the Sarkozy administration. One oversaw the civic board in Orleans, and one ran a theatre. I stood up at one point and spoke a little about myself. We ate and talked pop culture and the future of the middle class in France.

We listened to the guest of honour, who spoke about the long-term consequences of video games for our culture, and whether they will properly address our desire for social interaction. It was all very well thought out, all very benchmarky, all very stimulating – but not sexually. I was so relieved I wanted to kiss everyone there, but then I thought, 'John, don't push your luck.'

I joined not so much a secret society in Paris, but Paris society as a whole. It's only when I tell my friends in New York that I've joined a salon/lodge/reflection group/think tank that I get the clichéd response.

'You can call it what you want, John. We all know you've joined a sex club.'

CHAPTER EIGHT

WESH WE CAN

'C'ÉTAIT UN ENTREPÔT DE PISSE,' I reminded the realtor who'd come by to give us an estimate on our apartment one rainy day in April.

'*De pisse?*' she squinted back, looking every bit as revolted as if I'd just flashed her.

'*Oui, de pisse,*' I confirmed. '*Pouvez-vous le sentir?*' ('Can't you just smell it?')

I inhaled and opened my chest as if I were taking in air at the shore.

By then the agent had turned her back to me and was talking to Anaïs about square footage, subtly letting me know she didn't care much for my description ... that my apartment was formerly a 'warehouse of piss'.

What I'd wanted to convey, of course, was that our apartment had once been a warehouse *for spices*, and if I was fluent enough I would have said, '*en-trah-poe day peace*' (*entrepôt d'épices*) not '*en-trah-poe dub peace.*' The *day* and the *dub* were the stumbling blocks based on accents I had never bothered to learn in school or in France, and which are glaringly absent from my French emails, where I usually

WRITE IN ALL CAPS anyway to avoid all those accents, acute, grave and circumflex.

When people ask, I tell them I speak French like Arnold Schwarzenegger speaks English, meaning you *undahstand everyteeng* I say, but nobody thinks I'm French. And most Americans I know would gladly sign up for that. I get where I want to go. I can talk my way out of a jam. Some people even find me charming. But if you asked me fifteen years ago where I thought my French would be by now, I probably would have aimed higher – perhaps not Victor Hugo level, but definitely higher than *'All bee bach.'*

Like any good immigrant, my goal upon arrival in France was to become fluent; a term that, I realise now, has different interpretations. 'Oh, my God, you're fluent!' my American friends squeal as they stand next to me gawking while I just order a baguette. But that's not quite the full story.

At first, I just wanted to speak as well as Bibi. No better, no worse. And since I was arriving in France at the same time she was, me via Air France, her via Anaïs, she'd serve as a human benchmark by which to gauge my own progress. Hell, if anything I had a head start on her. I had years of French under my belt, and I knew how to study. Plus, I was smarter.

In a way, I was adhering to the writer Malcolm Gladwell's premise that expertise in anything can be achieved by practising something for ten thousand hours. If Gladwell was right, I thought, in ten years my French would easily be in the bag, leaving me to pursue other ten-thousand-hour endeavours, such as whittling or macramé.

I was also determined not to be like the other Americans I crossed paths with those first few years, the ones who told me they'd been here for decades, yet still hadn't assimilated as they'd expected they would. I'd find them in the touristy areas of Paris usually, drinking pints on the F. Scott Fitzgerald beaten path or in a café where Josephine Baker once sang, stuck in a time they didn't even live in.

These people seemed odd in many ways, one being that they were rarely chic. Most had grey beards and ponytails, and carried ratty backpacks while strolling the banks of the Seine in Birkenstocks with socks as if they were in Burlington, Vermont. Call me a stickler, but you'd think after thirty years of living in the fashion capital of the world something might wear off. Nope. They were happy as clams – looking as if they were still travelling on a Eurorail pass.

What separated me from these people, I thought, was that I was married to a Frenchwoman. And Anaïs's French, I might add, is really good. She speaks so well even French people are impressed. The pronunciation, the acceleration, the turning on a dime: she has it all. The way she could inflect her voice or drop the *passé simple*, the way she'd drive through difficult words like *serrurier* (locksmith) or *vétérinaire* (veterinarian) as if they were brush weed, then pull up with an old-school adjective like *revêche* (churlish) to describe another parent seemed, to me, magical. If anything, I thought, being married to her would be like having a virtuoso in the living room playing Chopin all day, and simply by listening I'd eventually become a maestro myself.

Why this never happened is anyone's guess.

One reason may have to do with a quality that many would consider an asset: I'm not afraid. I've never been one of those Americans embarrassed to talk because they think their French won't be understood. I'm more like the bad golfer swinging away, oblivious that his balls are slicing and braining people on the course. The swing *feels* perfect to me, so why is everyone ducking? Often, I confuse facility with mastery (if it rolled off my tongue with ease, then it must be correct) and take compliments as confirmations of my talent, not as people being painfully polite.

I also conveniently never compare myself to native French speakers, but instead to those American cretins, the ones nasally stumbling their way through another limited-as-hell sentence like '*Trump est... est... comment dire* soon to be impeached?' their accent sounding more and more like a kazoo being blown in your face.

Since I was able to roll an *r* better than the other guy and do the fancy twist of a tricky French transition word like *dont*, as in '*dont vous faites partie*' ('of which you are a part'), I never really buckled down to learn other specific grammatical principles or subjunctive uses, the stuff an advanced knowledge of French requires. I picked up bad habits, taking short cuts through phrases I knew were wrong but that I thought perfectly conveyed my point. I also tried physical gestures to reinforce what I was trying to say, instead of just phrasing things correctly. Once, during a case of stomach flu, I needed to tell the doctor *I'd been vomiting*, but instead of shifting into the imperfect, I used the present *je vomis* (I'm vomiting), then stood up from his desk and mimicked a fake retch. The doctor in question pushed back from his seat thinking it was the real thing, only for me to fake-retch again then say '*dans le passé*' (in the past), moving my arm as a way to signal time past. He quickly wrote me a prescription and handed it to me at arm's length.

Although exhausting, this way of talking has become the norm for me, and its Frankenstein delivery would forever betray me, no matter how quick my cadence.

French tourists looking for something in my neighbour-hood have stopped to ask me countless times where the Canal Saint-Martin or the Gare de l'Est is. And when I start giving directions, proud that I can be of help, they hear my accent and wave me off, thanking me cruelly, in English, of course. 'No, tank you. We find it ourself. Bye bye.'

Otto and Bibi are no different. When I'd pick them up at school, I'd say hello to their friends and try to crack a joke in a pathetic dad attempt to gain fifth-grade street cred, lacing some of my speech with slang I'd learned along the way. It bombed, of course, but what was more painful was the way Bibi and Otto cringed, embarrassed by their father's accent. Here I was thinking I was a cosmopolitan figure in their eyes, someone who'd lived in New York and Paris and wrote for magazines. Instead, to them I'm Luigi from Mario Brothers who says in botched English, 'I work hard for that you go to school! You will be beeeg success my *niños.*'

Meanwhile, Anaïs over time morphed from coach to crutch, one I'd use too often for things I probably could have explained, but didn't want to. I'd be caught up with some horrible technical support call, something involving the Wi-Fi router, the technician blaring on about a WEP password or a reboot button. But instead of gutting it out (which would have helped me more in the long run), I'd turn tail and run down the stairs pushing the phone in her annoyed face like a child whose school principal just called.

'It's the guy from Orange. He's explaining how to hook up the Livebox thingy.'

'Why do I have to deal with this shit? Can't you?'

'Please!' I'd beg, close to tears, pointing at the phone. 'He's waiting!'

I never wanted to admit I didn't understand. I never asked people to repeat themselves or to just slow down. Instead, I developed an impressive tic of laughing on cue or dropping throwaway expressions, such as, *'ah, bon?'* ('really?') or *'dis donc'* ('well, then') or *'vraiment?'* ('you're kidding me'), which gave people the impression I understood (which I didn't). They'd buy into my sham, taking it as a cue to speak faster, use more slang and subjunctive, and thus leave me to respond only with more *dis doncs* and *ah bons* and *vraiments*, all the time nodding and laughing and gulping wine, hating them for making me do something so strenuous.

And each time, without fail, there'd be that invariable fork in the road of the conversation. The person might be discussing something hideously boring like the French thirty-five-hour work week, starting with *'Une fois, il y a eu un type du bureau'* (Once, there was a guy from the office), but I'd forget the word *type* in this case didn't mean *kind*. It meant *guy*. And because of this, I assumed he was describing a *type of* office, not a *guy from* the office. The conversation soldiered on, my friend telling me this *type du bureau* was being *liquidé* meaning *fired* (liquidated), me off the reservation imagining a *type of office* being *cleaned*. When he told me his union was going to fight it, I responded in turn, 'Yeah. If anything, just ask them to clean it over the weekend.'

It wasn't until I'd reached the bottom of the staircase post-party that I'd realise why his confused face flashed pity. By then it was too late to clear things up, just as it was too late for the retort I wanted to make at another dinner the Thursday before or that incisive position I could have taken up at the lunch on Sunday had I understood that *faire le pont* meant *take a long weekend*, not *build a bridge*, in Provence. All of this 'passable' French I practised was a day late and a dollar short, and it always seemed to end with me at the bottom of a stairwell kicking a wall.

bfd bfd bfd

This wasn't the first time my French betrayed me. Twenty-five years earlier, I'd spent my junior year abroad in the town of Aix-en-Provence, and even then, I was learning the hard way that language can turn on a dime, word order can make you look like a fool, and the placement of one tiny insignificant letter can get you into hot water. Over the Easter holiday, my American friends and I took a three-day trip to Bordeaux, and our hotel room was burgled. When we made the declaration at the police precinct, I mistakenly told the gendarmes that we'd been *violé* (raped) instead of *volé* (robbed). I couldn't understand why they were so shocked by my story and kept insisting over and over that we'd really been raped. 'Of course we were raped! I was raped. They were raped. We were all raped! Why do you think we're here?' The women with me didn't understand much French either, so when the officer asked them if all this was true, they smiled and said *oui*.

Determined to not make the same errors this go-round, I started to bone up on my mechanics, riffling through Bibi's grammar book late at night, or buying some Rosetta Stone software, or reading the daily *Libération* out loud to Anaïs. But, as I gradually improved, I sensed French friends' disappointment. To them this improved French of mine was plastic surgery gone bad, and it was clear, after talking to me for five minutes, this new full-of-himself *quasi-fluent*

John was indigestible, frightening almost. It was as if I'd become a witch. They liked the older John better, *l'Américain* who could speak French – not another French guy. There were enough of them already.

And, because of this, they quickly lost patience with me, as if to say, 'All right, John, you want to play in the big leagues? Here we go.' They didn't slow down when talking about Derrida. They made references to fringe politicians and TV hosts from the 1980s, people I couldn't possibly have known. And, all of a sudden, I found myself back in the same place I'd been before – laughing and slamming back wine in between *ah bons?* and *dis doncs*.

The problem wasn't just the accent, though. It was context. No matter how well I could pronounce words or expressions, there was no *terroir* in my vocabulary. Words all meant the same to me – almost like those black-and-white letter magnets you stick to a refrigerator. *Table, chaise, connard, pute, vélo, merde* were all interchangeable and non-denominational, standing next to each other in my brain like a bad haiku. Since they had no meaning to me, I'd invariably say something I shouldn't.

Once at Bibi's birthday party, I pulled aside one of her friends, Gaspard, who was the same age as Bibi and who was struggling to clip together one of his Beyblade tops. Beyblades, if you don't know, are a Japanese invention, where your top is given a name and is constructed according to its power or speed, and they were the craze at one point in Paris.

'Gaspard,' I said. *'Ta toupie – elle est foutue, tu sais?'* ('That top of yours is fucked up, you know?')

Gaspard stopped and looked at me. He didn't know what *foutue* meant exactly, nor did I really, but simultaneously both of us sensed something was off. And not until Gaspard's mom swooped in to let him know that 'John speaks French as a *deuxième langue*' did Gaspard grasp that I was handicapped. Deep down, though, I think, I did know the difference and said the word anyway. Only because, for once, I wanted my words to have impact; to generate a reaction from someone, a change from my usual emasculated attempts to speak. Sure, it was extreme to call a kid's toy fucked up, but in a way, it made me feel whole again.

But what I actually said was worse. *Foutue* is the past participle of *foutre*, and in parlance it means 'ruined' or 'fucked up'. But if you look it up, *foutre* literally means 'sperm or vaginal secretion'. I'd been using *foutre* and *foutu* willy-nilly for a decade almost, not realising how often I was saying the word *sperm*. It's a miracle I'm not locked up. The more I thought about all the variations of *foutre*, the more I wanted to vomit. 'Fuck you' in French is *Va te faire foutre*. And it's a phrase I've used tons. What I now know I'm really saying is, 'Go shoot sperm on yourself.' Another John speciality is 'I don't care,' which in French is *Je m'en fous*. Literally translated? 'I'm shooting sperm on myself.'

At times, if I'm really angry, I might say, 'I really don't give a shit,' which in English isn't great but at least it's not '*J'en ai rien, mais rien à foutre*', which technically means (yes, you heard it right) 'I have nothing, and I mean nothing, to shoot out in terms of sperm.' How did Anaïs not crack up laughing when I'd told her 'I had nothing to shoot out in terms of sperm' if we got a parking ticket, or that 'I'm shooting sperm on myself' what someone else thought? And did these French parents know what they were saying when they told their kids to stop bullshitting them or to stop lying? Because I swear I just heard one mother say to the word, 'Stop ejaculating on my face, Oscar, and pick up your toys!'

This language my mother had always told me was the mother tongue of Voltaire and Baudelaire and Rimbaud was sounding more and more like the language of Pornhub.

I once asked Anaïs what the first sentence was that she remembers learning in English.

'Brian is in the kitchen.'

'Sorry?' I replied, looking over my shoulder to see if a man was actually standing there in our kitchen.

'No, *idiot*,' she reassured me. 'That was the first sentence I ever learned.'

'And the second?' I asked.

'Where is Jenny,' Anaïs said, 'the sister of Brian?'

Anaïs told me she remembers these phrases perfectly because Brian and Jenny always intrigued her. Were they twins? Why was Brian the only one in the kitchen? she wondered. And, more important, where was Jenny? Where was Jenny!?

I love listening to Anaïs's English, almost as much as I do her French. She has a solid base, sure, better than my French probably, but it is her hiccups that stand out, like when she asked if we could rent a *canooie* (canoe) on the canal over Easter, or when she'll repeatedly order carrot cake in an Elmer Fudd accent, pronouncing it *cowit* (carrot) *cake*. She'll also sometimes mix British words into her jargon, such as *jumper* to describe a sweater, or use old-fashioned words like *trousers* to show me what she just bought at Zara.

I've learned a lot about French indirectly from Anaïs, especially in the questions she poses to me about English, questions I find petty only because I never know the answer.

'What's the difference between *I could* and *I might*, for example?' she'd ask. 'Or between *shouldn't* and *shan't*.' When I told her I didn't know, she didn't believe me, because for Anaïs, the rules of language are set in stone, and if you don't have rules, well, you don't have a language. Saying 'It's just like that. You just say it that way' doesn't cut it.

And now I know why. French is a complicated, rule-obsessed mess, and it's been that way for a while. In 1685, France created *L'Académie française*, a council that has overseen the preservation of the French language throughout the centuries. *L'Académie* is made up of forty members ranging from historians, to poets, to novelists, to philosophers and scientists, all called 'immortals'. Meetings are held once a week in private, and once a year in public (the first Thursday of December), and each member wears a long black coat with swanky green leaf motifs. Every member enjoys Supreme Court judge-type tenure, meaning they go on until death.

L'Académie serves as the official arbiter of the rules and usage, vocabulary, and grammar of French, compiling new words each year for an all-encompassing *dictionnaire* that's been published only nine times since the late 1600s. None other than the president of the République himself is the 'protector' of the institution. Many have credited *L'Académie* with helping the French language to evolve while maintaining a fundamental link to the past. This, they say, has allowed France to preserve its culture while other countries have watched theirs washed away by globalisation. Others say *L'Académie* is a conservative institution that has made French sexist, obtuse, full of contradictions – what the French love to call '*poétique*'.

I realised this poetic-ness the first time I read one of my own pieces translated into French, because my first reaction was 'Who is this pretentious asshole?' The text was fluffy and built to impress. There were lots of round-about descriptions and tissued phrases and metaphors referencing French things I'd never heard of. Plus, it was peppered with nauseating *jeux des mots* (puns), which you often find in headlines of French newspapers, puns I wasn't smart enough to come up with. There's a special embarrassment one feels when you know people are reading what you wrote and finding it pompous. It's like looking out your window and realising the entire block has been watching you play air guitar in your bedroom. (This has happened to me.)

Reading French John made me realise I could never master this language. This was the writing of some pretty boy in the west of Paris wearing yacht shoes and a sweater tied over his shoulders. France wasn't helping in my pursuit of the language, either. Each year, Anglicisms, it seemed, were cropping up left and right in the French lexicon, like a whack-a-mole game. And I'm not just talking about *le chewing gum* and *le weekend, le coming out* and *le fist-fucking*, English words the French have conveniently co-opted simply out of laziness.

There are verbs as well; English verbs actually, but with an -*er* tacked on at the end to make them seem French. At the Apple store near Opéra, I was told to *rebooter* my computer in order to *uploader* my files to iCloud before I handed it over to them for repair. And at the co-op meeting, I was asked whether we were planning to *boycotter* an owner's plan to renovate the ventilation system. Bibi even asked if I would *liker* her photo on Instagram and become one of her *followeurs*. You heard it right – *follow-eurs*. And sometimes the English words were used incorrectly. Hip parties were called *hype soirées*, and if a guy was a loser, you were told he was '*la loose*' – they'd spell it with two o's and an s but pronounce it *looze*. Odd.

It also seemed like anything or anyone trying to position itself as young or modern had to have some English in it. I saw in a recent magazine a list of leading *start-ups* (yes they say start-up) design firms in France: Be Dandy, Brand Brothers, Bug, Coconuts, Creative Room, Curious, Future Brand – and that was just to the F's. Restaurants near us opened with names like Blend and Flesh and Big Fernand. A microbrewery on the canal was called Paris Brewing Company (PBC). There was even a British fish and chips joint called The Sunken Chip. All in Paris, all near me, all making me mad. I told a friend recently if I were ever to launch a start-up or a business, I'd make sure to go as French as possible, something like Jean-Claude Bernard et Associés. That to me would be edgy.

Despite the tsunami of English flooding in, French society was doubling down on its effort to build a wall to keep it out. French cinema and French TV continued their age-old policy of obliging networks and studios to dub shows and movies instead of subtitling them, which in the case of a series like *Duck Dynasty* doesn't really make much sense. If anything, it creates chaos. The way the dubbing works is the English version remains, but at a lower volume underneath the French version. This means the viewer listens to a character explaining how to shoot a crossbow in hillbilly American only to be shouted over two seconds later by someone speaking proper French. Two voices run concurrently and neither is synced to the character's lips, so if you understand both languages your brain explodes.

Advertising hasn't been spared this French protectionism either. Any poster in the metro or at bus stops that features something written in English at its top, something very difficult to understand, such as *U le Boss*, has to be followed by an asterisk, which means there's a French translation waiting for readers at the bottom. I've never noticed people scratching their heads, looking perplexed at these posters. Nor do I see them bending forward and squinting at the small type along the bottom, *Vous, le Patron*. In just the same way a voice comes right after the credits for the reality show *Le Bachelor* (The Bachelor) and says sotto voce '*Le Gentleman célibataire*', these French posters and dubbed shows are meant to convey the message that 'Yes, English does exist, and we're going to pretend like it doesn't.'

ɞ̶ɩ̶ɮ̶ ɞ̶ɩ̶ɮ̶ ɞ̶ɩ̶ɮ̶

Around this time, I can't really say when, I regressed. Like an adolescent who suddenly starts playing with dolls again, I began to fake like I didn't understand French, just so people would slow down or take care of me, or both. When I called the bank, I'd press the '2' button on the menu 'to speak in English' as an act of protest. In the past, if Anaïs and I argued, I'd battle her French to French, going toe to toe. Now, though, I threw in the towel, getting off my chest what I had to say in English, and when she'd come back at me in French I'd quickly deflect what she said with a shrug of the shoulders and that cop-out line 'I have no idea what you're saying.'

To compound the problem, I began forgetting my English. Over a summer vacation with American friends, I shocked everyone when I asked if I should put out the *cutlery* for dinner. Things were made worse when later that week I pronounced *hammock* as *hom-och*. Something had gone horribly awry. In an attempt to become bilingual, I was slowly becoming Jean-Claude Van Damme ni-lingual.

Anaïs and I had agreed two languages should be used at the house. She'd speak to the kids in French and I would use English. But, for them, English was a pain in the ass. Nobody spoke it at school. None of their friends spoke English. So what was the point? Better to help Dad out with his French, they said, which obviously needed tons of work. And at first I was forgiving. I didn't want to add to their already cluttered minds. But, after a while, a mild form of insanity grabbed hold of me. When no one I spoke to in English would respond in English, I'd be haunted by the impression that nobody was listening to me; that I didn't count, and that I might not even be alive. Since it was apparent my English had no jurisdiction, I started scrapping it midstream. A 'Bibi pick up your towel!' would be met by *'Mais je n'ai pas envie, Papa!'* ('I don't feel like it!'), to which I'd respond, *'Mais ramasse ta serviette tout de suite, merde!'* ('Pick up your damn towel now, goddamit!') The fact that she'd immediately pick up her towel showed me how counterproductive English had become in the house. And, since I wanted a clean apartment more than bilingual kids, I kept going in French.

Soon, however, the children were responding neither in French nor in English, but in something called *verlan*, a Parisian form of French slang spoken backward, with syllables reversed much as in pig Latin. The name *verlan* itself comes from inverting the syllables of the word *l'envers*, which means, of course, 'inverse'. Asking Bibi *'Who are you texting?'* would be met with *'Ah t'es chelou, Papa!'* which meant 'Stop being *louche* [bizarre, heavy], Dad.' But the word *louche*, in this case, gets thrown into the chipper of *verlan* and comes out *chelou*.

Half of Bibi's and Otto's words are like this. *Fête* (party) became *teuf*. *Chez moi* became *chez ouam*. If friends were black they weren't *noir*, they were *renoi*. And if they were *Arabe* you had a choice. Either you used the early *Verlan* from the 1960s and said *beur* or you could choose the remixed *verlan*ised version of *beur*, which was *rebeu*. I am told you can generally tell the age of the person by which version of *verlan* they use.

The list of words open to *verlan* is bottomless, and often the *Verlan* version comes from a word that's *already* slang. In the case of a police officer, the slang version has been *flic* for decades, but with *verlan*, it's *keuf*. If you have a girlfriend, she's not your *femme*, because that's too old-fashioned. You say *ma meuf*. And yes, it's a lot cooler to say *ma meuf* than *ma petite amie*, which puts you back in the 1940s.

Although Anaïs's French will one day be housed at *L'Academie française*, she, too, understands *verlan*, and has no trouble understanding Bibi and Otto. Sometimes she'll even speak it, and seeing her do so is like watching her breakdance all of a sudden, a way to show the kids Mom still has it.

If you live in France long enough you realise the French never really say *oui* like we think they say it. More often than not, they pronounce it *wayh*, and it's usually with an inhale, as if they're talking while taking a drag on a cigarette. (Which is also most often the case.) '*Wayh, pourquoi pas*,' your friend might respond when you propose to meet him for drinks. '*Wayh, je crois*' ('Yeah, I think so'), you'll hear from someone who's not really listening to what you're saying.

The only time I hear *oui* pronounced *wee* (the way I learned in class) is when the French say it with exasperation or out of annoyance, as in Anaïs saying '*Oui* [weeee], John, I turned off the stove!'

But what I heard from Bibi and Otto during *la rentrée* (the back-to-school period each year) of 2015 had nothing to do with *oui* or *wayh*. They were saying *wesh*. But it wasn't even to respond *yes* to a question. *Wesh* was more a tack-on word to something said before.

T'es nul wesh (you suck, you know), Bibi would remind Otto at breakfast.

Ta gueule wesh (shut up, okay?), Otto would then respond while slurping his cereal.

Wesh could also be 'of course'. *Mais wesh, Papa, I have swimming class today. I always have swimming on Tuesdays wesh.* Or it could mean 'all right!' as in *Wesh, those Jordans are slamming wesh.* Wherever or however you want to say it, *wesh* has taken over the French language and has become the most emblematic expression of urban French. If you listen to a conversation of young kids in my neighbourhood, it's possible you may hear four or five *weshes* per minute. It's in every rap song. Most reality TV stars or soccer stars drop *weshes* here and there, and over one summer in Boston, we even overheard preppy French kids saying *wesh* in front of us at the ticket counter at Logan Airport.

Wesh, I learned, is a derivative of *oui* mixed with the Algerian and Moroccan Berber expression *ach*, which means *what!* I love any word that combines *yes* and *what* simply because that's basically my motto – *Yes… wait what?*

Nobody born before 1980 uses *wesh*. And if you do, you sound ridiculous, kind of like those forty-five-plus dads picking up their kids at school and trying to be cool. *Wesh* has been ushered into our house with myriad other words I never would have thought would work in France. There's *swag* as in *T'as le swag, Papa* (You've got swag, Dad!) or *thug* as in *Oh le thug!* (Check out the thug!), but Otto and Bibi pronounce it with a silent *h* so it comes over as *tug,* as in *tugboat,* which, of course, makes me laugh, almost as much as it does when they pronounce *Facebook* 'Fayceboooo*k*' or *Instagram* 'Anne-stah-Grum'. Then there's *bledard,* which means 'nerd'. *Bledard* comes from the West African expression *bled* (pronounced *blehd*), which means 'small town'. Basically, if somebody's a *bledard* in Paris, he has small town tastes, and doesn't understand what's cool. And to make things even more insane, Otto recently called me a *darblé,* which is *bledard* in *verlan.*

Thanks to all of this *verlan weshness,* I've fallen back in love with my French. Maybe because, for me, it is the real French – the French I've always gravitated toward – a language made from and spoken by immigrants like me. Plus I understand it better than most of my French friends, and so have a chance to upstage them. One can't place a value on that.

But *wesh* stirs up a strong reaction in people, beyond what a playful modern slang word should. In a way, *wesh* is seen as worse than a curse word, because it seems to mark the invisible line between those who use it in their everyday speech and those who are properly educated. How parents of some of the kids I see using *wesh* could ever think their Jean-Christophe is going to be mistaken for anyone other than a rich smartass is beyond me. But the French sensitivity about *wesh* betrays just how tenuous the grip of proper French is over the pecking order of modern society.

Sometimes I wonder if the French response to *wesh* that I sometimes see comes down to our complicated feelings about culture, class and race. Maybe there is a parallel between the way France won't allow itself to appreciate the *wesh* richness the country has to offer and the way it sometimes undervalues the vital contributions millions of immigrants living here have made.

For her twelfth birthday, Bibi hosted her first *boum* (pronounced *boom* but spelled with the letter u, and don't ask why). *Boums* are starter parties for French adolescents and pre-adolescents, and they're dry runs for what to expect in the next six decades of socialising with the opposite sex: mixed dancing, gossip, crushing rejection, elation, fear, shame and, somewhere in the corners of all this, you hope, fun. Yours truly was asked to DJ, which means I was simply a chaperone who helps out if there's a technical difficulty, but I'm not supposed to touch the music, ever.

Bibi's playlist featured the usual suspects: Nicki Minaj, Beyoncé, Rihanna, but the song that brought everyone to the floor, even the boys who'd been sitting on the side hiding their shyness by making fun of everyone, was MHD, a skinny twenty-two-year-old from the Cité Rouge projects in the Nineteenth, who's become the *it* rapper in Paris. In a way, MHD incarnates the disconnect between real France and official France. His eponymous album *MHD* seemed to be everywhere; in the street on those Bluetooth portable speakers, inside passing cars, on cellphones in the metro and, of course, on YouTube, where his *clip* (video – pronounced *kleep*) had more hits than the population of France, more than any known French pop star, and more than all those national treasures like the late Johnny Halliday or Charles

Aznavour combined. And yet, not shockingly, he still wasn't considered a mainstream success in France.

What I love about MHD is that he always refers to Paris as *Paname*, an expression that reaches back to old-school crooners like Edith Piaf and Léo Ferré. He's also tapped into the current habit of young kids who refer to their neighbourhoods by the first two digits of their zip code. If you're from Paris, you're from the 75 (*le sept-cinq*). If you're from the rugged north-east suburbs of La Corneuve, you're from the 93 (*neuf-trois*). There's a moment in one of MHD's songs, 'Champions League', when he gives a shout-out to the various corners of Paris, in an easy-to-remember verse that everyone, even I, can follow and pronounce.

And it was during this moment of the party, me with the laptop trying to be invisible, watching all these sweaty mixed-up kids from the Tenth shouting out their *sept-cinqs* and *neuf-trois* and *sept-septs*, that I realised my story with the French language had come full circle. I'd arrived here with the hope of mastering classic French only to walk away with a twenty-first-century version, one found on Snapchat, in schoolyard insults, and on posters with asterisks; a French that's part English, part *verlan*, part *Wesh*, part *Brian in the Kitchen* and fully French, sung by a kid from a nearby neighbourhood and repeated by a new generation of *boum* attendees, who shared, in some way, his story, his city and, of course, his language.

It was also during this party that I recalled one of the visits my mother made to Paris. It was during the lead-up week to our wedding, and she and my father invited Anaïs and me out to dinner in the Marais to celebrate. When the waiter approached and asked if we were ready to order, I turned to my mom to do the honours, expecting her to shine in French just as she had years ago when I was a child.

When she started to speak, though, I realised Mom's French wasn't all that good. It was broken a bit and lopsided. There were too many *uhs* and *pardons*, the pronunciations were off. She didn't really roll her *rs* like I'd remembered. And by the time she botched the escargots, I realised the fluent French I envisioned Mom speaking had never been that fluent at all. But when I was a child, what she'd conveyed to me in her stories and speech was a love of place and people, of colours and ambience; probably much in the same way my American friends see me today when I order those insane baguettes and almond and pistachio dessert cakes from the 150-year-old boulangerie on our street.

And it's moments like these that have taught me what it truly means to master a language. It's where the pride and love you have for your home comes through with an ease and dexterity and, *wesh*, a fluency that's all your own – even if you do speak French like *Ahnuld*, and the walls around you smell of piss.

CHAPTER NINE

WILL YOU BE MY FRENCH FRIEND?

ONE OF THE THINGS I TOOK AWAY from studying abroad is that there's no guarantee it will work. There's a real chance you'll come back to the States not speaking French at all. Parents, of course, don't know this. They assume the boots-on-the-ground immersion and their son's or daughter's youthful ability to pick things up will more than do the trick. And they're happy to fork out the money to make it happen. Little do they know it's more likely their child will return fluent in hash smoking or consequence-free sex than French-speaking. At least that was the case with my program. So much so that our host town of Aix-en-Provence was coined 'Sex-en-Vacances'.

The reason fluency isn't a given is that life isn't fair. The classroom can only take you so far. There's pre-season and regular season and, as players of all sports will tell you, the speed's just not the same. What happened in the petri dish of my study abroad program was a horrible irony. Those who slaved over grammar and vocab in class but who stuck socially with their University of Wisconsin crowd came back with substandard French. Unlike the bubble-writing platinum blonde Shannon, who landed the French boyfriend.

Shannon identified value in the market place on arrival, realising the most important thing to do was to not just make friends, but make *French friends*. French friends were Monopoly properties like Boardwalk or Park Place or the railroads (which we all know you need to have), assets that would pay off big time if you played your cards right. The Swedish pal or German hanger-on were nice and all, but you were never going to get anywhere in French with them.

French friends became part of Shannon's vernacular, and she'd name-drop them any chance she had: 'Well this weekend, I went to Marseilles with my two *French friends*,' she'd brag at one of the program's start-of-the-year mixers. 'And they brought some of their *French friends*, too. And well, it was just sooooo French.'

When she'd introduce you to one of her catches, she'd do it in a garish way, as if the person's Frenchness were a job title, like attorney. 'John, have you met my French friend, Philippe? He was born and bred here, French as French comes. Ain't that right, Phil?'

I was never sure what the French friend was getting out of the deal. Being paraded around like a Marc Jacobs bag must have made him question whom he'd just become friends with. Yet I probably underestimated his ulterior motive – learning English from an American woman.

I was neither a nose-to-grindstone studier nor a socially savvy blonde, but I made up for it all by being a virtuoso at table football, or *le baby-foot* as it's known. And it was during countless games in the student lounge just off of the auditorium where I was supposed to be attending lectures that I made *my* French friends and learned to communicate.

I was never that discerning about the French people I met. I assumed I was the one who had to prove himself. And whereas after five seconds with an American I could tell if we'd click, I had to give more leeway to the French kids I'd meet just to bridge the culture gap. If you were French, you could have been a racist snob, but I wouldn't know. In fact, the French speakers I ended up being closest to weren't actually French. They were Moroccan. And although their French was perfect, they, like me, were studying abroad that year and looking to make friends, which in right-wing-voting Aix wasn't easy.

Once exams wrapped, I was invited to Casablanca, where one of the fathers was the satellite dish king, and given a sham office job distributing mail. On weekends, we'd road-trip to the casinos of Marrakesh. And while my fellow Wisconsin Badgers were spending the rest of their summer travelling with other Americans to Interlaken or Bruges, I learned how to sell a satellite dish called a *parabole,* order a vodka tonic to the dance floor and scream to a pack of Moroccans from a sunken velour couch, *'Plus on est de fous, le mieux on rigole mon bébé!'* ('The more the nut jobs, the better the fun baby!'), which made them all gasp with laughter, probably because I sounded like Borat before *Borat.*

And that was fine, too. Because I was speaking! And when I came back to the States, much to my parents' delight, my French was better than that of anyone else in my program; well, except for Shannon's, of course.

🏮 🏮 🏮

When I married Anaïs, part of the dowry she brought to the table was her wide selection of *amis*, which, by marriage, I was allowed to use. This was exciting, because I hadn't yet outgrown the reflexive desire of wanting French people to like me. It also meant I wouldn't have to scrounge around at the American church for buddies, like other expats, leaving pathetic Craigslist-type announcements on the corkboard ('Do you want to speak conversational English in a relaxed environment in exchange for French lessons?').

Anaïs was okay with letting me play with her friends – 'but only temporarily', she said. 'Until you get on your feet and make your own.' She wasn't kidding.

The varied life Anaïs had up until we met gave me a wide range of potential friends to sample. As a teenager, she lived for a while in a posh suburb called Ville-d'Avray right outside Paris near Versailles. There she'd made preppy friends who voted right, but had club memberships and liked to drink. Later she'd majored in political science, got the equivalent of an MBA, and worked in advertising, so the friends she made during this time were quick and witty and knew what stuff like 'bad optics' meant. And now that she worked in opera and theatre, there were actor and singer friends, one more eccentric than the next.

Following our wedding, we began receiving invites to *dîners* (dinner parties), and for two years, I felt like a debutante coming out to society. Each week, it seemed, Anaïs would announce a new line-up of dates. 'We're invited to the Guilberts this Saturday and the Ariels will be there, plus the Terasses want to know if we're free next week.' I was forever running to the barber to get my hair trimmed or to the dry-cleaner's to get my shirts pressed. At thirty-two, there would be no more *baby-foots* to shine at, though. If I was going to make French friends, these *dîners* were my only opportunity. So don't blow it, I told myself. And while I primped my hair and cuffed my pants, I allowed myself to imagine the prospect of Anaïs's friends liking me. Maybe we'd become real friends like the ones I had in New York. Perhaps I'd make them laugh in French as I had my pals in Casablanca. We could take long Parisian walks together in Père Lachaise discussing death and Hegel. Or we'd have private talks in the stacks of a bookstore in the Marais, my new friend confiding to me that he'd made a horrible mistake, that he'd accidentally killed someone and needed my help.

'I'm not sure where to turn, John,' he'd whimper.

I'd tell him to calm down (in French), that it was good he'd come to me first. 'I'm your friend, Jacques,' I'd say. 'You can talk to me … in French.'

But to get to this herd of wild buffalo grazing in the sun-dappled field just out of shooting range, there was a tricky river that needed to be crossed – the *dîner* itself, which, to me, was full of dangerous currents and hard-to-see eddies. These were intricate affairs – marathons that demanded a keen understanding of table placement geography, guest invitation, and the sophisticated and meticulous *dosage* of ambience, music, soft drugs and, of course, good food.

If I could pull it off, I'd be set, I told myself. Hell, we could even eventually host at our place and make it *the* convivial carousel of social networking for years to come. But if I tanked, dear God, if I tanked. I'd be back at the American church posting sad announcements in the entryway.

🍾 🍾 🍾

Like any good athlete preparing for a big game, I started out by watching films. And in particular a series on French TV called 93 *Faubourg Saint-Honoré*, a weekly reality show devoted not to cooking, but to the *dîner* itself, shot and hosted by Thierry Ardisson. Each week, stars wanting to plug their upcoming film or book or album would arrive at 93 rue du Faubourg Saint-Honoré (Ardisson's residence), punching in the code of the building's front door, buzzing the apartment from the *rez de chaussée*, then arriving *chez* Thierry with flowers and lots of *bisous* to go around.

The show started in the kitchen while the chef was preparing the meal and where Ardisson, with his husky Parisian accent and the look of an FBI bureau chief, would sit his guests at the prep table, offering them a glass of champagne or a kir while he texted or spoke on the phone with late-arriving guests who were either lost or asking (which I always do) who'd already arrived. Again this was in real time with nothing edited – no fast-forwards, no cut-aways. After fifteen minutes of watching *93 Faubourg Saint-Honoré*, you realise that if you're not in Louis Malle's *My Dinner with Andre*, dinners are probably best left unfilmed.

Ardisson spiced up the show by sometimes inviting stars with chequered pasts. He'd even go so far as to ask some of them over the *apéro* what it was like to have a twenty-gramme-a-week coke habit. I liked this sort of drama, and I let myself imagine those at the table were secretly feuding with each other or didn't know the other had been invited. Some would spend the night staring ahead, icelike (boring), or actually answer the coke habit question (not boring). Sometimes people would drink more than they should and not be as funny as they thought they were (which I found hilarious). Some might leave early. Some might argue, and *93 Faubourg Saint-Honoré* killed in ratings.

The more I watched, the more I picked up on the little things Ardisson did: his ability to keep the conversation moving by including reticent guests; the way he kept them in the kitchen at the beginning and talked them through the food; the way he poked fun and massaged egos while simultaneously doling out the *confit de canard*; and how he was always conscious of who had an empty wine glass. The fact the show was appointment television in France meant something. The institution had weight. There was a way to host a dinner, and Ardisson, for me, was a natural.

If dinner parties weren't on TV, how to properly host one was a constant topic in magazines, where titles like *Côté Ouest* or *Elle Décoration* would devote entire issues to the subject, describing it as *l'art de la table*. Sometimes the magazine would take you on a culinary voyage around France, the table setting being the jumping-off point to promote the latest Baccarat crystal wine glass release or matching tablecloth and napkin. Cutlery could not be overlooked, either.

I myself had written one of these kinds of pieces for *GQ*, focusing on Perceval, a small knife manufacturer which had been fabricating knives for hundreds of years and supplied them to three-star Michelin restaurants around the world, all from an atelier in Thiers, a small village in the middle of France's nowhere. The standard Perceval knife, the 9.47, I was able to tell readers, was a masterpiece of utility and elegance, and when you held it, something old crept into your wrist. There actually was a perfect weight and sound to the knife, though a set of 9.47s could set you back. It was, however, positively affordable when compared to the high-range Percevals – the knives geared toward Russian oligarchs whose handles were made from meteorites. Yes, meteorites. From space.

But the moment I truly grasped how seriously the French took their *dîners* and the kitchens to prepare them in was when I found myself at Ikea. There, while glancing through the Billy shelves and the Poang closets, I noticed hundreds of people on high chairs hunkered over computers, looking as if they were filling out job applications. Anaïs told me they were using Ikea's construction software to conceptualise the kitchen of their dreams block by block, cabinet by cabinet, weighing in on where the cutlery would go and how the pots and pans would fit into the lower cabinets. It wasn't unusual for people to spend hours at these computers, and then return the next day to soldier on with colour shades and wood choices. These people were not rich – just Ikea shoppers prioritising. And, unlike many I know in New York or LA who have Sub-Zero fridges and granite islands and Wolf stoves, these French people actually cooked in the kitchens they were designing.

Like many of those at Ikea that day, Anaïs knew our kitchen would be the fulcrum of our apartment and social life. But unlike most of her compatriots, she envisioned it sitting smack-dab in the middle of the action, which, in our warehouse meant the garage where the trucks were still parked. Anaïs stalked around this space, kicking up dust, walking off paces in a way only French people can, who know how long a metre is. '*Cuisine ici,*' she pointed to her right. '*Cuisine américaine, bien-sûr,*' she winked back. *Cuisine américaine* meant an open kitchen with a central island, a concept that, in 2002, the French hadn't yet embraced. Most apartments we visited had kitchens five-minute walks from the dining room, a vestige of the Baron Haussmann days when the food was cooked by staff, hence the secret stairwell linking the kitchen to a *chambre de bonne* upstairs.

🍾 🍾 🍾

Before hosting *chez nous*, I'd spent months gaining intel from all our friends' dinners, and what struck me was how much time we had to fill. The *apéro* or cocktail alone could take an hour, probably as a way to allow for stragglers. Unlike Americans, who, if you tell them dinner is at 8pm, buzz your apartment at 7.59 or 8.01, the French take their time. Some will show up at 8.40, some at 9.00, some even later than that. And it's not frowned upon. Paris offers a multitude of excuses. Kids need to be tucked in. Finding a parking place can take an hour. Plus there's a subtle game of payback in play. If people come late to your dinner, you're allowed to be late to theirs. It only means more champagne for those who arrived on time, or a chance for your host (like my friend Guillaume) to usher you into the kitchen to show you the duck he (and now you) are going to pluck or the octopus he's about to extract the ink from.

But the extravagant meals and decorative tables aside, what made my friends' dinners shine was how the hosts managed to find that sweet spot between formality and ease; the way they'd take your coat, fetch their angelic children to say hello, all while managing to monitor the soufflé and hand you a glass of champagne. They made multitasking look chic. They were gracious, but not patronising, and when it was their turn to talk, I'd listen to their French purr like a turbine, then glance around the table in astonishment that no one but me seemed to realise how good the fucking wine was.

I was also doing things I'd never done before in the States, like enjoying a five- to ten-minute break from the table mid-meal. The French call this a *trou normand* (Norman hole), a pause one takes between the second and third dish to smoke, catch the score of a game, or drink a shot of Normandy Calvados to break the rhythm and get your sea legs back. 'Why a Norman hole?' I asked my friend Paul-Henri as he and I belted back shots of Calvados in the kitchen. 'Because the *Calva* is burning that extra hole in your stomach to keep you eating.' He was right. I returned to the table a new man with a lighter stomach, as if just booted in the bathroom, and was ready to rally.

The *trou normand*, like many things I was discovering, would never work in the States. There's just not enough time for such luxuries. Often, when I feel full and need that mini-pause, there's someone passing me a dessert or there's a smiling waitress badgering me while I still have food in my mouth. 'How's everything goin' there? Still working on that?' he or she will ask, me throwing back a big two thumbs-up to confirm that, yes, I was still working here.

'Why do they say this?' Anaïs asked once as our New Hampshire diner waitress walked away.

'Say what?' I asked, quickly swallowing what I normally would have finished chewing.

'If we're *working* on it. Why do they use that *verb*? Do they think eating is a job?'

Anaïs had a point. We'd just dropped the kids off at summer camp and were on our own for two weeks, lobster rolling our way around New England. 'Working' was what we were trying not to do, especially over dinner.

It wasn't the first time Anaïs had opened my eyes to these American expressions I've taken for granted, another being 'quality time', a concept that infuriated her. 'Are we quantifying time now, too? Does certain time have more value I don't know about? Has it come to that?' she'd ask me in bullet points, always pronouncing QT in bunched-up pieces – *KWAL-IT-EE TYME* – exaggerating each syllable.

🍾 🍾 🍾

When our apartment was finished, it was this *KWAL-IT-EE TYME* that pushed us to hold our *pendaison de crémaillère*.

(Hanging of the *crémaillère*, which is slang for housewarming party, and is a medieval word used to describe the metal racks that hung over the fire and to which you attached a boiling pot. Back in the day, if you told people you were 'hanging your *crémaillère*', you were cooking a meal, namely a meal for others. And it was from this expression, I assume, the notion of the dinner party started.)

Our version had its first-game jitters. I learned I didn't know how to properly cut cheese (diagonally, not horizontally, and never vertically, meaning from the front of the wedge to the back – except for Brie), and that it's frowned upon to sit couples next to each other. I also found out you don't start eating until '*Madame est servie*' (the 'madame' of the house has taken her seat and is served), then things move to the left of Madame. '*Madame est servie*' is one of these old-school traditions that is laughed at but followed religiously. It's so mainstream, it's also the French title for the 1980s Tony Danza sitcom *Who's the Boss?* Who knew?

But our party wasn't a failure. And, in the years to come, as more plates passed and Perceval knives clinked, our confidence grew. Soon Anaïs and I made up a Martin and Lewis or Crosby and Hope dinner party duo, she playing the straight man (always the harder role) and me the clown, stepping on phrases and taking two *trous normands* just to impress. Our dishes would take on a creative boldness. We broke out my parents' old wedding plates, and during all these occasions I found myself not only listening to, but participating in, French debates on French subjects, to the point where I could trash a French celebrity or learn about a murder nearby and say in slang, 'No fucking way! Here?'

What our dinners may have lacked in the sophisticated choreography of our friends' affairs, we made up for with American panache. Neil Young would play in the background a lot, or we'd skip the formal table setting and eat off *ze island*. We'd serve stuff the French usually don't eat, such as ribs, stuffing, yams – basically Thanksgiving meals each time we hosted. Our guests left giddy, and I was proud. We'd found our social groove, and I felt like a proper American in Paris – a cosmopolitan *homme de lettres*.

I also like getting hammered.

And in the process of making all these new French friends, America started fading into the distance, looking rushed and tedious. Having a social life in France didn't seem daunting any more. Hell, just look at all the dinners we're having and all the French friends I was making!

🍾 🍾 🍾

Armed with a confidence I hadn't felt since Sex-en-Vacances, I blossomed into a modern-day George Bailey from *It's a Wonderful Life*, strolling through my neighbourhood in the Tenth as if it were Bedford Falls. A day wouldn't pass without my chatting up the tailor or the pharmacist, anyone who might want to be my new French friend. If you followed me on a walk to the metro, you'd hear me spouting *bonjours* and *ça vas* as if I was handing out campaign flyers.

'*Salut, Jacques!* You can keep the bills.' (mailman). 'Hey, Rémi. Those new Vélib bike rentals? Boooo!' (me giving the thumbs down to a bike repairman). 'Mr Lallier! Starting early on that *vin blanc*, are we? Can't say I blame you!' (old pensioner at the café). A trip to the butcher could turn into a long chat about PSG's prospects or whether Paris had too many bus lanes, or my divulging a back issue that had flared up, Bibi watching incredulously, wondering how her father had become so intimate with these people.

'Why do you talk about yourself so much, Dad?' she'd ask as we left the cheese guy, me making it a point to smile and wave to others across the street.

'Because I can, Bibi,' I'd respond. 'Because I can.'

The problem was that, in all this excitement, I failed to realise how full of shit these smiling overtures of mine were. And apparently, those I chatted with didn't realise how full of *merde* I was, either. As a result, signals got crossed, and invites I didn't expect to receive soon began piling up; invites Anaïs looked at as one would an invite from the local Scientologists. 'Who have you been talking to now?' she'd ask me, exhausted to hear that the neighbour down the street (whom she'd already IDed as a person to avoid) had asked if we were free next week for dinner.

'You know you really have a ... *syndrome,* I think.'

Anaïs could have used the word *problème,* but instead chose *syndrome* because she needed to convey to me how fucked up this *disease* of mine was, a disease that forced us to accept yet another random invite from another rando she didn't want to know that well, but had to, because her husband couldn't help himself. She knew excuses could only work for so long, and eventually we'd find ourselves at dinner out of obligation.

There was the *'dîner des artistes'* (artist dinner) hosted by a woman (we'll call her Eloïse) who fashioned herself as a poor man's Peggy Guggenheim and wanted to have artists at her table so they could discuss art and be eccentric and treat her like the benefactor she wasn't. Our respective CVs had apparently convinced her that Anaïs and I fit the bill, and as the dinner painfully limped along I remember only two things. The guests were insane people. There was a man who was convinced that the iris of our eye is the exact replica of how the Big Bang explosion looked, and that we carry the Big Bang with us every day. The guest who wasn't crazy was an actress. I recognised her because she'd appeared in a *Seinfeld* episode, which, of course, I mentioned at the table. This was met with silence by everyone, including the actress, who simply glared at me. Sitcoms for this crowd were a low form of art, I guess.

☗ ☗ ☗

I had to finally admit that Anaïs had a point about my 'dining with strangers syndrome' and so we declared a moratorium, keeping to ourselves for much of the next year. Which, of course, created its own problems. When friends noticed they weren't receiving an invite *chez nous*, they doubled down on asking us to their place, paranoid we were either angry with them or having couple issues. This, in turn, led to more declinings, which then led to more invitations.

'How about we meet for drinks after work?' I'd propose. Work drinks had served me well in America. It came from a time-honoured American tradition of keeping friends without having to go all-in. But, with Parisians, these invites routinely fell flat, met invariably with the response 'But, John, what will we eat?' 'Nothing. We're drinking. That's the point,' I'd respond, a bit annoyed I even had to explain.

For my French friends, a drink without eating is close to heresy and borderline suspicious. My long sabbatical from the social circuit must be for a reason. Maybe I was single now. Maybe I'd come out. Maybe both. 'What does John want from me with these drinks?' I saw them asking themselves as they stared at my text in their cubicle. 'Could it be sex?' The French didn't like the spontaneity part, either. Socialising involves more than just being social. They want a two-week heads-up to give them time to think of a tasteful dish and time to order that case of wine from the vineyard they loved in Burgundy. Plus, they always wanted more time with us – time, time, time, time – which beers and pretzels over a game at a bar won't give them.

Fine, I said. Dinner it will be. But just when I felt ready to dip back into French society, putting quality ahead of quantity this round – meaning just close friends and not all the time, the unthinkable happened: Trump was elected, and suddenly I didn't have an appetite. Dinner plans were scrapped and invites turned down. I couldn't bear seeing anyone, and nobody, it seemed, could bear seeing me. If I wasn't shutting myself in the house out of shame I was forcing myself to make those neighbourhood rounds again, as a way to salvage the wreckage of America's standing in the world. Yet every post-election interaction felt gross – like a thirty-second political anatomy class, me forced to explain for the n-teenth time why the liver of the Hillary campaign had so many spots on it, or why people ignored the white working class or if the Russians really did have a pee tape.

The *bonjours* I received now were different from before. They carried in them either open hostility – 'I see you across the street, John. *Bonjour*, John!' – or perverse curiosity. People wanted explanations. *Pourquoi*, John, they'd ask. *Pourquoi* people in America were not going on strike? (The French would!) *Pourquoi* the Congress would let this man do what he was doing? *Pourquoi*, John? *Pourquoi?* But instead of giving people the in-depth answer a supposed 'journalist' should have, I froze.

Suddenly I was the one who was proposing an olive branch dinner *chez nous*. 'Sure,' they'd respond, 'but not this weekend, though, nor the one after.'

Anaïs felt the most cheated. She'd done nothing wrong, and now she was married to a man with the social status of a registered sex offender, a man shuffling around in slippers reading Trump's Twitter feed.

'Can I have my friends back, please?' she asked finally. She was calling in her debt.

'By all means. Take them!' I told her.

There's a point in every expat's life where you hit a wall. Where the role you think you've been playing living in a foreign land is just that, a role. I wasn't John, I was learning, but *Djohn*, a manufactured Euro version of what I thought played better abroad. And those who had claimed to be my friends wanted a minstrel American version of me; someone happy to play the foil to that stereotype. These people had befriended me, sure, but for the same cynical reasons I had them – to have *un ami américain*. Maybe all of these dîner-havinga and French-friend-schmoozing was nothing but a sham masked as cultural assimilation.

If Anaïs wanted a party, because she wanted back her friends, then fine, I'd give her a party. But I'd do it my way – a July Fourth barbecue with all the Trumplandia trappings these French fuckers could eat. As the date loomed, I chucked all I'd learned from Thierry Ardisson. I filled up a plastic baby pool with ice and beer and worked on a playlist that featured lots of country music. I didn't bother to give out the code to enter the building, nor did I specifically mention a firm starting time. Figure it out, I thought. People can come when they want, I said. Bring kids. I don't care. And no. There's no table placement. Just a big buffet and some cornbread. Don't know cornbread? Don't come, then. And when I made these rough demands in a semi-polite email that started with 'Since you don't want to have work drinks...' I was sure nobody would come.

Then, on the big day, with my ribs ready and my Merle Haggard playing and my father's World War II American flag hanging in the living room, I waited with my feet up in the garden, which explains why I didn't hear the buzzer. Anaïs did, though, and drip by drip, people arrived with wine or flowers or both. Faces I hadn't seen in years came through the door. There was the Turkish tailor, Mr Gulak, who'd accidentally cut my suit trousers into shorts because his wife didn't understand my French. There were the school moms and the wine guy and even Marie-Laure, the fellow dog walker I couldn't bear small-talking with any more, because she always had some stupid petition for me to sign.

The *bisous* flowed, and so did the champagne. Everyone picked hors d'œuvres from *ze island*, each skewering a pig in a blanket with toothpicks decorated with tiny American flags. Gone was the choreography I'd admired at French dinners past. *Madame wasn't servie*. Madame was drunk. Our apartment was an exotic wonderland of kids running pell-mell and hot dogs cooking, a dog barking and Kid Rock blasting. And the French, who I'd assumed would detest this uber-American party, were loving it. This was the John they'd been waiting for, the John in his element, a bear released from the circus touching snow for the first time.

As the night went on, instead of the national anthem, we held sparklers in the garden and sang Stevie Wonder's 'Happy Birthday' in a way only the French can do, with an *OPPY BAIRTHDAY TOOO UUUUU!* There was an air of resistance in the air, and those around me embraced my stiff, awkward body to let me know they understood my pain. They'd just suffered an election themselves that almost voted in Le Pen. We danced and clinked our glasses, and as we formed a limbo line to Jay Z's 'Empire State of Mind', I yelled to all my new/old/reconciled French friends, *'Plus on est de fous, le mieux on rigole, mon bébé!'*

CHAPTER TEN

COUNTRY LIVING

By the time Bibi turned nine and Otto five, I'd dug myself into a Parisian dad rut. I'd done every museum Paris had to offer, every aquarium, every zoo, every stroll through every square, every shop at every Saturday market, not to mention having every conversation possible with every other stupid alterna-parent with a stroller and sippy cup along the Canal Saint-Martin. Whether it was linked or not, my health had been failing, too. There was a period where it seemed I was on antibiotics every other month for bronchitis I couldn't kick. The antibiotics were efficiently and routinely prescribed by the SOS Médecins, the French roving doctor who, yes, actually comes to your house at any hour of the night for free.

After fifteen years, it still remains a giant mystery to me how *SOS Médecins* is at all possible. Each time I call, I expect to get a disconnected message, and each time they knock, it feels like Christmas. I scamper down the stairs like a kid, often forgetting I'm actually sick. And sometimes I'm not. I just call *SOS Médecins* to boost my feelings about having chosen to live in France.

'Look, Anaïs! He has that old black leather bag and a stethoscope, too!' I turn back to look at her, wide-eyed.

'And this cheque I give you for forty euros,' I ask the doctor each time before he leaves. 'I'm reimbursed at the end of the month, correct?'

He nods and I giggle, asking Anaïs to pinch me again.

The only downside to *SOS Médecins* is that they prescribe amoxicillin for anything more than a cat scratch, in my case preferring, I assume, to nuke whatever's going on inside me so they don't have to return in three days to witness me mince around the living room again. And I'm actually fine with that. It's gotten to the point where even if a doctor starts prescribing anything homeopathic at first, I'll stop him mid-write-up with a 'Why waste time? Let's just bring out the big guns, shall we?'

As the Paris dinner parties wore thin, it occurred to me that, while I loved our friends, I would like to see them in larger doses. I was tired of getting the PR firm version of their life over a three-hour dinner; the career conquests, the many wins and few losses, the kids shining at school stories. I wanted forty-eight hours embedded, where by the second day they're happy to tell you where their life went off the rails. And the French, I might add, are willing to give you that. They'd just rather tell you in the countryside, so when you shriek in astonishment, the neighbours won't complain.

And, no, I wasn't looking at the country as a way to get back to basics. For me, the country wasn't where you toiled the earth or lived a subsistent, noble life. It is where you created. My mother's family owned a farm outside

Pittsburgh, but she rarely picked up a hoe. Instead, she painted on easels while my grandmother made stained-glass windows and welded steel sculptures. Aunt Louise, the 'acclaimed artist' in the family, would drop by once a week to paint them painting. Nobody cared two bits that the cherries or pears around them were dropping and rotting. This was what you did on a farm, a philosophy handed down by my great-grandfather, F. C. Murdoch, also a painter. He'd bought the place in the late 1800s to pursue his craft and painted prolifically until mental illness forced him to retreat to the garden, where he finished his days cutting the grass with scissors.

When Paris got rough around the edges, I'd allow myself to envision leading a similar country-gentry idle life – one where I'd change into my city clothes once a week and take the train into Paris for the day. Maybe in the morning I'd see my lawyer for an update on my various business concerns, then follow it up with buying a hat. I'd share a two-bottle lunch with a writing *compère* in a tiled bistro somewhere near the Montparnasse station, where he'd complain to me about deadlines and how editors were giving his pieces *humour-ectomies*. I'd stare back at him with pity, wish him good luck, then hotfoot it back to the train and the countryside, where warm soup awaited me.

Anaïs's vision of countryside life was less romantic, probably because she'd grown up in a family that owned châteaux and knew the perils of roof repair and septic tank installation and lawn maintenance and rural isolation, stuff that lurked in the shadows of all this bucolic bliss I fantasised about. She was also, rightly, suspicious about the idea of countryside communing. For, in France, country houses are often what are called *maisons de familles* (family houses), places where nobody lives full-time, but which are calendared up by various cousins, uncles and second cousins, each of whom owns a 10 per cent share, and all of whom constantly fight over the prime dates for usage. The ones who have the February dates bitch that the June date holders should pay more. And the May daters won't go unless the April date people have de-winterised the house at their own cost.

The reason that most of these houses have remained in a family for so long has less to do with family pride and more to do with the houses being unsellable. Not only are they expensive to maintain and renovate, each usually has ten or more owners who all have to agree on a measly price. And, if you stand to receive 10 per cent of not so much, you may just choose not to sell, assuming it's more chic to say 'My family has a house in the Pyrenees' than to buy a mid-range mountain bike.

For estate planning purposes, *maisons de familles* also tend to be tangled up in perverse French legal arrangements where the house is left to one kid and the *droit de l'usufruit* to the other. *Usufruit* is a word I love because it looks like *use your fruit,* but it's pronounced like 'use it free'. And it literally means that. *Usufruit* is the term describing the right to use property, even if you don't own it, for free! Not only is this the coolest coincidence word I've ever come across, I see it everywhere in France, even in the minutes of our co-op meetings. In our apartment building in Paris, there's a terrace that belongs to the co-op although it's attached to our neighbours' apartment. And, although our neighbours are the only ones who have access to the terrace, it's the condo's responsibility to maintain it, meaning we pay if there's a leak, we pay the taxes, but only they can use it... for free!

Deep down, though, what pushed me most towards the idea of country living was that I wanted to become the male

Mimi Thorisson, an American expat living somewhere in the Médoc region, whose idyllic life has become a much-followed blog and bestselling book full of healthy lifestyle tips, thoughtful cuisine (country stew with a stock drawn from her own vegetable garden), multi-kid delegation, refined clothes and stone chimneys, alongside a professional photographer/husband who captures it all.

If Mimi could do it, so could John, I thought. Which, of course, turned out to be wildly off the mark. For, as euro-cultivated and continental as she looks, Mimi, I can tell, from her Swiss-watch efficiency and steel-eyed optimism, is deeply American. I, on the other hand, with my half-assed compromises and defeatist outlook since acquiring this money pit, have become mediocrely French.

Before I go any further, I feel I need to make a point here. Publishers, on occasion, should take out liability policies on books they think might pose dangers to readers. Sure, it's just a book, but sometimes books lead to ideas, which then lead to actions, which could lead to disastrous consequences. Books are more dangerous than swimming pools. Peter Mayle's *A Year in Provence,* is a case in point. The bible of expat living, it gassed up the head of every Anglo-Saxon male, convincing him that, if all else goes to shit, he could always move to the French countryside, buy an old farmhouse and start fresh.

The area Anaïs and I chose for our own country living experiment was a piece of Normandy called Perche. Two hours southwest of Paris, it straddles three *départements* – the Eure-et-Loir, the Orne and the Sarthe – all of which form a bigger region called Basse-Normandie (Lower Normandy). An ancient fiefdom in the fourteenth century, the Perche no longer exists in legal form. It's as if eastern Tennessee, western North Carolina and southern Kentucky called itself Rocky Mount. People may say they're from there, and you might be able to find a T-shirt with the name on the front, but you won't find it on a map, birth certificate or driver's licence.

I'd stumbled upon the area as part of a last-minute panic-induced February vacation that ended with us renting an apartment in a tacky timeshare golf resort, a thing Americans know how to do fairly well and the French do really poorly. Although the insides were a sham, outside there was a mysterious February fog that lingered into the late morning. Cows grazed over Scotland-esque rolling hills, and there was a light drizzle that felt clean as a church suit. I also slept well for the first time in years, the kids rode ponies, I wasn't coughing and, for once, I could walk around without feeling molested by Paris.

In July, we rented a house nearby, this time for four months, the idea being that we'd pass the summer in the countryside instead of taking a three-week vacation like all the other schmucks. And since the rental was close to Paris, we'd have the luxury of returning to the city, if need be, for work. The French actually have a word for this, *villégiature*, so that summer we told people we weren't going on vacation but choosing to live instead *en villégiature*. It sounded chic, kind of like the way certain East Coast people use the word *summer* as a verb.

On the lease, I saw that our village was technically a *hameau*, meaning hamlet, a French word I love because it fitted our house so well – a thin, eighteenth-century Normandy farmhouse called a *longère*, where the barn and the stables are all under the same roof and where Frodo Baggins could have lived in his early years.

Although that summer was somewhat of a disappointment weatherwise, the autumn was pleasant, and we'd made enough friends and planted enough flowers and gotten the lay of the land enough that we decided to continue renting for the rest of the year, just to see what it would be like to spend Christmas there, and if we could survive unforeseen stuff like heating bills or rodent infestations.

I'd learned from the rental agent that our house was a bizarro form of *maison de famille*. The owners weren't French, but British expats who lived most of the time in Africa. For them, the Perche was a summer destination while it was winter back home, and Normandy, they said, was close (kind of) to England, where their children lived.

Judging by their names, Prudence and Rupert, and all the books about hedge growth and variations of grass and floral composition that stood on the shelves, not to mention the immaculate state they'd left our garden in, I took it that the owners had green thumbs.

As part of a gentleman's agreement separate from the lease, we agreed to lend them the house for three weeks to a month each year and, like worker bees, Rupert and Prudence would transform the backyard, allowing the grass to grow knee-high-wild in parts, but with a pathway through the patch for the children to run through. They'd cut the hedge short at certain points, allowing you to gaze over the hills and into the valley. They brought in rhododendrons and wisteria and azaleas and, by the time they'd leave, our backyard looked like a tasteful outdoor living room – one we'd eventually trash.

Because unlike Rupert and Prue, who had time and talent and patience, I had thirty-six hours each weekend, and I was damned if I was going to spend that time trimming trees. Instead, once a month, I'd jump on the tractor an hour before departure and drive wildly over the grass and flowers, leaving a scorched earth of patchy zigzags behind me.

And each time our British landlords returned, I'd cower behind them watching Prudence's face turn white. 'What happened to my garden?' she'd say, looking out over the Golden Globes actress I'd just given a bowl cut. They'd find all their garden trowels and rose-cutting gloves in the garage, staring back at them like untouched china. And I was okay with the frowns, only because I knew Rupert and Prudence would not only bring the garden back up to snuff by the time they left, but they'd fix all the leaks and deal with the broken appliances – stuff I would myself inherit when I bought the house from them a year later.

Friends told me we'd made a smart decision to buy a country house, not because they thought of it as a great place to relax, but because it could come in handy when the shit hits the fan in Paris. And considering all the social unrest and terrorist attacks these past years, I'm starting to think maybe they're right. One friend told me Paris could last only 2.4 days without a replenishment of food and water, confiding to me over the weekend (they always confide over the weekend) that he has a survival kit stowed away in his basement and a three-pronged exit strategy to leave Paris if need be.

'But you can't walk to the Perche, so get that out of your head *tout de suite*,' he told me. It had never occurred to me to walk to the Perche, but I let him continue anyway.

'It would take four days minimum, and where are you going to get water. Huh?'

My look showed him I had no answer.

'And if you do have water, others are going to want it.' He gave me one of those self-satisfied winks and moved on to the topic of gun ownership.

I've been told by other friends that I should hire a *sourcier* (well finder) to find the old well that's surely out back somewhere. Others have advised us to start a *potager* (vegetable garden) just to make sure we'll have something to eat once the state collapses. On separate occasions, I've been instructed where to collect rainwater, where to set up solar panels, how to make a bee colony and, of course, build some extra rooms where my survivalist friends could sleep should Day Zero arrive. All this 'end of days' planning can make it hard to relax over the weekends.

In a crazy coincidence, it turned out that one of our new neighbours in the Perche shared the exact same name (first and last) as Anaïs's father. We made his acquaintance at a Midnight Mass at the local church on Christmas Eve, and later visited his home to meet his wife. It wasn't clear if they were the famous usurpers I'd heard about, but what was certain was that they'd done quite well for themselves. They had a family château near our house, which was owned by the elder brother, who was something like the governor of the region. The supposed-usurped name carried great weight now. In fact, it caried a good deal more weight than it had when it had been wielded by the 'old' branch, as I observed to Anaïs.

Seeing its benefits, I began to float Anaïs's family name in the Perche. I signed the bill for the electrician in her last name. I gave the grocer her name for a delivery. Eventually even the French-fry-stand guy at the municipal pool knew my new last name and, of course, assumed, since my family was also the governor's, maybe he could get a new stand next year? I'm not proud of it, but I responded, 'We'll look into it,' and my foreign accent made the claim seem legit. For them, I was the German branch maybe, a Count von Hohenlohe or something or other.

I was having a ball. And no, I didn't have qualms. If anything, it was payback-usurping, something I considered fair and above board. I'm sure if I was French, I'd blush each time I used Anaïs's family name. But being American meant it was water off a duck's back. I felt I'd been given licence to play with something others took super-seriously and looked at it as a rare reward for having to file two tax returns, for all the misunderstandings at our condo owners' meetings, and never knowing if I'm cutting the Brie correctly.

Of course my karma wheel would soon turn when I then became embroiled in the sordid affairs of other locals. Six months after we closed on the house, our twice-a-month cleaning lady called me in a panic. What I gathered through the blubbering over the phone was that her husband had written a cheque from my chequebook, which had apparently been left in the living room cupboard. I told her to calm down, letting her know this wasn't the end of the world, that she'd done the right thing to call, all the while casually asking how much she thought the bad cheque had been written for so I could call the bank.

'Sixty thousand euros, John.'

'I'm sorry,' I squeaked, 'I don't think I heard you correctly.'

'*Soixante mille!!*' she cried.

Her husband, the story goes, had used her keys to enter our house and had taken a cheque. The weird thing (and what made this a far from open-and-shut case) was that he didn't steal anything else and he never tried to cash the cheque. Instead, he took an inordinate amount of time whiting out my name and my bank's name, replacing it with his own local bank's name, sloppily and even handwritten in places. The goal, I'd later learn, was to show his wife and her family that his drunken gambling days were behind him, and that he had, in fact, the wherewithal to be a solid upstanding husband moving forward. 'Look! I've just been issued a bank cheque for *soixante mille* to prove it!' The problem with this 'bank cheque' was that it was so cheaply doctored that anybody could have seen it was fake, even his wife.

To add to the insult, I found a couple of photocopies of the cheque on the glass of our photocopier, which meant he hadn't just taken the cheque and scrammed. No, he stayed here, perhaps even into the night, probably hunched over the dining room table, making a couple of photocopies here, Stanley-knifing something there, whiting out something in the corner there. Maybe he even browsed fonts before taking a break to go through our drawers, never fearing in the slightest the possibility of someone coming home.

Since the cheque in question was more or less a prop used in a lie, I didn't think of it as that heinous a crime. My bank did, though, and when I called to see if anyone had cashed a sixty-thousand-euro cheque on my account, they were more upset by my blasé attitude than by his act.

'Monsieur von Sothen,' the employee stuttered. 'The fact you call us so late is concerning. Of course, we never would have cashed it. You have nowhere near those funds. You know that.'

'I do know that,' I replied. 'And thanks for reminding me.'

Following Chequegate, I became something of a legend in town, as the story took on a life of its own. One version had me with a couple of uncashed sixty-thousand-euro cheques lying around and the thief taking one of them. I surely didn't help my cause when I nonchalantly joked to a neighbour weeks later, 'Can you imagine the balls? That's almost a month's salary, for crying out loud!'

Buying a country house showed me first-hand why the French often call the rural parts of their country *La France profonde*. Although *profond* means *deep* in this sense, I always read it as *profound*, as in profoundly poor. Now, rural France's misery isn't on the scale of, say, Appalachia. You don't have widespread addiction to OxyContin or meth labs or higher-than-average infant mortality. But you can go to the E. Leclerc, France's mega supermarket chain, and find yourself with a full shopping cart behind a mother with three screaming kids buying a tin of paté and a two-litre Fanta.

A lot of political attention is paid to what the French call the *désertion rurale* of France, people fleeing the small towns. Industrial displacement, outsourcing of jobs, and a flight to the cities by young people have seriously affected places like Lower Normandy, and considering agriculture is France's third largest export behind aviation and pharmaceuticals, many are now worried.

The reforms implemented by agricultural minister Stéphane Le Foll – allocating 300 million euros to boost agriculture in struggling areas, 75 million to create ten thousand new farmers and doubling the budget on organic growing – have yet to bear much fruit (no pun intended), partly, I think, because Le Foll looks too much like Javier Bardem's character in *No Country for Old Men* to be taken seriously.

In 1998, the Perche became a *Parc Naturel Régional*, which gave it protected status from urban sprawl. The development laws have become super-stringent, work permits have to pass a jury in each hamlet and a housing code similar to Nantucket's has been implemented, meaning that, for instance, the shingles of each roof have to be a certain colour. For this reason, the Perche, although relatively modest economically, has appealed to a certain Parisian looking to flee the city but weary of the touristy Gucci bling in towns on the Normandy coast, such as Deauville or Honfleur.

According to Monsieur Letour, who owns the cows next door to us, this preservation has come with a price, though. The lack of industry has kept the cost of living down and along with it the price of his beef, while the costs of raising the cows (the grain, the rent, the machinery) seem to rise each year. Letour may be suffering, but he still spares no expense for his wonderful cows, and I've grown to love having them next door to us. They roam in groups over the hills surrounding our house like Mardi Gras floats. Over coffee you'll see white masses passing through the trees as they graze in the east at sunrise, then find them lounging in the setting sun on the opposite side of the house, staring at us blankly as we moo back at them over cocktails.

The cows are so dependable, they've become my sundial in troop form. You can look out during the day and guess, simply by where they're positioned, what time it is. Ironically, they've also become, for me, the ultimate argument for vegetarianism. We've seen calves born in stables over the winter frolic in the spring grass like puppies, and groups of cows gallop like horses to greet my dog, Bogart, at the fence on Friday evening.

Two years in, we discovered they're of the Charolais breed, meaning they're not milk cows, but (as one of the *paysans* from the town told me as he brought a knife to his throat) beef cows, and I've done my best to keep from becoming attached on a personal level. Each has a number on its ear that looks like a tag from a dry cleaner's. '#1706, you are so cute!!!' says Bibi. 'Where is your friend #5609?' Otto asks. I don't have the courage to tell him. The only cow that maintains a constant presence year in, year out is the bull, whom Otto has christened *Couilles Man* (Ball Man), in honour of his enormous package, which swings in the breeze at sunset, and which I must admit is quite mesmerising.

I've learned that these grass-fed cows, although bred locally, aren't necessarily eaten locally. When I asked Raymond, the man who cuts our grass, which butcher he usually went to ('The one in Berd'huis or the one in Bellême?'), he looked back at me as if I'd just asked him which Starbucks he preferred.

'We split a pig at the beginning of the year with the Martins – then stock it in the freezer. That's my butcher.'

It's not that the locals look down on me, they just have no time for my input. Once I left my car at the local garage to be repaired, and while I handed the mechanic my keys I also offered up my theory of what could be wrong.

'How about everyone just stay in their lane? It'll be done next weekend when you arrive … from Paris.'

Other times, they'll give you a bullshit excuse and dare you to call them on it, simply because they know you'll do nothing in the meantime anyway. Once I called the electric company to find out when they planned to take down a giant electric pole that had been sitting in our garden since they changed the grid and put up taller poles down the road. The person on the other line responded, *'Aux beaus jours'* ('When it's nice out').

A certain generation of Percheron folk will, on occasion, talk to you in the third person, which is unsettling for someone like me, who can't even get his *tus* and *vous* correct. I learned this from Raymond in one of our first dealings, when I hired him to cut our lawn over the weekends we weren't there. *'Il était content avec la tonte?'* ('Was he happy with the cut?'), Raymond asked after the first job. *'Il revient la semaine prochaine?'* ('Will he be coming back next weekend?')

Not only did the conversation look curious the first three or four times, with me glancing over my shoulder each time, assuming Raymond was talking about someone else; but it also made me uncomfortable being spoken to like some squire. What made things worse was that I started responding in the third person, assuming it was protocol: 'Yes, he's very happy with the cut.' 'Well, yes, he's considering coming back in two weeks.'

Raymond found my responses bizarre, especially when I'd point to myself and say *John*, as if he couldn't understand otherwise. As our third-person conversations became more intimate, I soon began confiding to Raymond. 'He is somewhat sad, John, because the magazine cut a lot of the good stuff from his piece. They cut it just like that,' and I'd make a snipping gesture, 'without asking me ... er ... John.'

'C'est dommage,' Raymond would reply, pulling out his chainsaw and drum of gasoline.

'Oui, c'est dommage.' I'd shrug, heading back to the house to see how many people had liked my recent Facebook post.

It took me three years to realise the locals don't really care too much about my life in Paris, which hurts, because I assumed they'd find it interesting. And considering all the questions I pose about their livelihoods, the least they could do is return the favour.

I know I can be overly curious at times, and it's true, I have a pathological need to keep a conversation flowing. But every time I'm chatting with a local, it seems I'm the one doing the heavy lifting. I've gone hours having the complexity of forest ownership explained to me, who cuts where and when to seed, how to change fan belts, or how to inherit the right to moonshine Calvados.

The only thing, I've found, that my neighbours are interested in about me are my *malheurs* (unfortunate events). I'm not sure if it's because they're something they can relate to or if it's just some homemade anti-Parisian schadenfreude. But, fortunately for neighbourly relations, the *malheurs* are not uncommon.

Last year, for example, we were the victims of what's called a '*surcharge électrique*' (electrical overload), which happens when too much current passes down a line, subsequently cooking everything electric in the house (in our case, the fridge, the oven, the stove, the works). *Surcharges électriques* have resulted in houses actually burning to the ground, which sounds completely crazy and unacceptable to Americans, but is met with shrugs in the Perche.

We discovered we'd been *surcharged* over the October vacation of *Toussaint,* and our week of enjoying the falling leaves and headless-horseman costume-making transformed into one big insurance claim, collecting serial numbers, finding warranties, calling agents and retrieving new Wi-Fi routers (which I think was the worst). But when we complained to our neighbours, expecting sympathy, all we got in return was jealousy. 'Wow!!! Now you can work that insurance!'

Indeed, when the news circulated of our situation, everybody suddenly wanted to talk to me. 'Could I put my TV on your insurance claim, John?' Mr Dupont asked. 'Or at least my broken iron?' In the Percheron's eyes, insurance is held in the same respect as a lotto scratch. You pay each month with the hope that someday something will go haywire. No, our neighbours never go so far as to start a fire to collect on a ratty house, but if something – fingers crossed! – happens to the kitchen grid, it's time to cash in.

The only neighbours who sympathise with my *malheurs* are a group of other Parisians who'd moved to the Perche full-time. Sergei and Solange, for example, who had converted an old mill into a hotel and sound studio where they housed rock groups and recorded their albums, much in the same way the Rolling Stones cut *Exile on Main Street* in a dilapidated French château. When I first met the two, they'd just bought an abandoned elementary school, which is now a bar/restaurant and where I relive the days of drinking on school grounds. Another member of the transplants is Pascale, who works on studio films and lives in the Perche between shoots. Her friend, Agathe, runs a select showroom out of her house, while selling the same fashionable wear in a cutting-edge boutique in the Marais.

Also among this group are César and Anatole, who have gone full *Taliban organic*, buying land, seeding the field with their own grains, making three varieties of bread and growing vegetables according to season, and then selling it all once a week on Friday at 5pm out of a one-windowed shack in another nearby hamlet. The line of people eager to buy their wares is an improbable-looking group considering the surroundings: circus jugglers, dreadlocked white girls with Bugaboos, and the always smiling Theo, who bought a donkey to ride into town. If you happened to pass at the right hour, you might think the line outside was of people entering a party at *Vice* magazine. I cringe to admit that I often find myself in this same line, marvelling at how ironic it was that we'd all come to the French countryside in search of quality *terroir*, only to find ourselves buying from the sole local farmers who don't use seeds from Monsanto, Roundup or pesticides – Parisian hipsters.

I've found in the Perche that most people choose to drop by unannounced, which for a city person was considered tolerable in the 1980s, but nowadays just isn't done. If someone knocks at our door in Paris unannounced, I look at Anaïs frantically, asking, 'Are we expecting someone?' In the Perche, I'll know a car is approaching by the crunch of the gravel, and my blood will run cold, because I know I'm trapped. 'They've seen the car,' my mind tells me, 'they know you're here.'

Sometimes it's the electrician, Monsieur Duval. Other times it's the neighbour Georges with his kids, who want to play with our kids. Sometimes it's Raymond or the cleaning lady, Chloé. Everyone, by the way, has my phone number. Nobody, by the way, ever uses it to give me a heads-up. Sometimes they want to be paid for work done the previous month. Other times, they're just bored. And the cruel part is, they never drop by just for five minutes.

'No, I'm good,' Raymond will say, when I invite him in for a coffee. 'I just want to show you where I put the peat moss.'

'Now?' I'll ask, still in pyjamas, looking out into the rain.

'Would you prefer I come back later?' he'll ask, knowing full well the answer.

So there I'll be, in pyjamas and boots, staring at a pile of peat moss in a light 8am drizzle on Saturday, acutely aware that all my friends in Paris are sleeping soundly.

These casual drop-ins have become so systemic, Anaïs asked Santa for chic pyjamas last Christmas, 'So at least when we receive people, we'll be respectable. 'On the other hand,' she added, 'we can't really blame them. We're usually in pyjamas until two.' She had a point.

As payback, I decided to drop by my neighbours' house without calling, only to discover it wasn't much of an imposition for them. Raymond and his wife, Hermine, happily welcomed me in, sat me down and offered up some homemade *pommeau*, an aperitif that tastes like liquored apple cider, a Calvados, but not as harsh. By the second *pommeau* we were strolling through Raymond's *potager* talking about François who was chased by a wild boar last winter and the French TV celebrity who lives nearby and managed to piss off all the farmers by insisting on landing his helicopter in their fields, thus scattering all the seeds they'd planted.

'*Quel connard!*' ('What an asshole!') I yelled, a bit too loudly, a sign the *pommeau* was taking hold.

They asked me if I knew this star, and I lied and said, 'No, but I know someone who did and *effectivement* [in fact] he is a *vrai connard*.' We all laughed, and soon I felt guilty for having dreaded their presence, remembering, on my way back home, my car stuffed with lettuce and carrots and a giant pumpkin Raymond had given us, to have some *pommeau* on hand when (not should) they repay my visit.

What we all share, my Parisian brethren and I, is the love/hate relationship the locals have with us. Since we possess a certain buying power, they're forced to tolerate us up to a point. But if it was up to them, they'd prefer to buy and sell only to each other and leave the city slickers out of things altogether. That said, when they do attempt to sell to one another, it's at horrible events called *vide-greniers* (garage sales), which are constantly organised from town to town.

When I first attended a *vide-grenier*, I fantasised I'd stumble across an old silver set or a vintage workbench, only to be confronted by a post-apocalypse scene of broken-lawnmower blades, car batteries, half-finished motor oil tins, piles of T-shirts, *Cars–The Movie* bathroom slippers, and plastic baby bathtubs full of Will Smith DVDs. What I thought would be a bucolic afternoon of 'antiquing' transformed into being teleported back to 1929 right after the Crash or to somewhere in Bucharest in the 1970s.

Parisians stand out in places like this, not because we share the same frown of disappointment, but because we're wearing those giant Wellington boots, looking like forty-year-old Paddington Bears. 'You can tell Parisians in town, because they're the only ones wearing those boots,' an old Percheron told me once. I asked him why the locals didn't wear boots *en ville* (in town) like we do. 'We wear boots at the farm or in the stables where they're supposed to be worn. When we go to town, we're civilised.' I looked down at my muddy boots that I'd planned to track all over his store and nervously rubbed them onto the entryway mat.

I used to enjoy village chitchat like that. But now I live in fear, especially of the hardware store owner, who always seems to have a racist joke he's sure I want to hear – probably because the last time he told me one, I smiled, not understanding what it meant.

It was New Year's Eve, and my schoolgate friend Fred and I had just bought a set of cheap champagne glasses when, at the register, the owner began the joke's set-up. I should have known something was wrong, because I could see that Fred was wincing in wrinkled pain and staring at his shoes, wanting to leave. It was only later, back at the house when he translated the joke back to me, that I understood his pain.

'John, do you still like the *pine au noir*?' the hardware man had asked, which to me sounded like Pinot noir, but in this case literally meant *pine* (dick) *au* (of a) *noir* (black man). What made even the hardware store owner pause was how I responded on the spot ... with a big smiley 'I do indeed! *Glug glug*.'

When Fred saw how mortified I was, he tried to ease my shame and anger with a toast. 'Nothing rings in the New Year better', he clinked my glass, 'than being tricked into feeling you're racist.'

In February of 2016, there were regional elections held throughout France. The Front National (FN), the previously fringe far-right party headed by Marine Le Pen, had done surprisingly well, which sent media pundits and political prognosticators scrambling to explain why, how and who was to blame.

The centre right bemoaned the socialist government's handling of the French economy, whose stagnant growth and crushing taxes they said had stunted the middle class and pushed them to vote FN in protest. Those on the left blamed the centre right, whose cushy relationships with corporations and efforts to neoliberalise an already fragile French workforce had pushed the French worker to the protectionist warmth of Le Pen's *No to Europe* message.

Rural France had spoken, and our neighbouring town, I found out later online, had narrowly voted FN. This was a watershed moment. It was like that movie *Dogtown* by Lars von Trier, where Nicole Kidman's character, a city girl on the run, tries to win acceptance within a small village only to realise the residents are uniformly horrible.

The lone thing that made me happy about the election was that it confirmed a theory of mine I call the *boulangerie index*. The theory posits that the better the bread, the more racist/reactionary the *boulanger* is. The more amiable the *boulanger*, the more average the bread. Why my index only works for boulangeries, and not butchers or cheese guys, I don't know. What I do know is that our village's bread is really good, and it's created a giant ethical conflict for me ever since the election.

Not many people know about the Perche, even within France. Every time I tell people where we have a house, their first response is *'Où?'* While they know the Normandy coastal region or the Loire Valley, they've never been to the area in between. Hence I was surprised to find an old *New York Times* piece on the area in which the writer calls it France's 'last *Terroir*'. For the most part, the piece was spot on. She described the oddity of the Perche's anonymity among the French and the *Alice in Wonderland*-type rabbit hole trails formed by the tall hedges, but there was one factual error.

Yes, on paper the Perche is two hours from Paris, but the traffic is so bad on Friday night leaving and on Sunday night returning that anything two hours from Paris is inside Paris. Once you have a country house, you live in constant fear of traffic. You've either concocted ten different itineraries or you've created a convoluted recipe of metro to train to a car parked near the train station, which, in the end, gets you door to door in the same amount of time had you driven in traffic. Everyone is convinced they have the *white whale* itinerary to beat all others, one passed down from a friend of a friend who researched it over years, and which they will gladly text you and which you gladly curse while you're cruising at twenty miles an hour through an abandoned mall near Versailles wondering where the fuck you are.

I've experimented with different departure times, sometimes leaving Normandy at ten on Sunday night and arriving in Paris at 1am to lug Bibi and Otto out of the car in their pyjamas and up the stairs only to be greeted by a hernia. On other occasions, we'll leave at five on Monday morning to make sure the kids are at school by eight, only to have Anaïs and the kids abandon the car in traffic and take the metro the rest of the way in.

Closing up the country house isn't a picnic, either. Around 3pm, you start the evacuation process, turning off the electricity, emptying the fridge, boarding up the windows, cutting the water, bringing all the chairs in from the garden so they don't rust, throwing the laundry together for Paris in a garbage bag so it'll fit in the car, climbing into the car with another garbage bag of actual garbage that you'll drop off at the dump on your way home, and then get stuck in traffic with everyone doing the same Sunday-night routine.

And when you get to Paris, all the negative parts of city life become suddenly amplified at the *Périphérique*. The Tenth sometimes feels like a slightly upscale Calcutta. There's trash everywhere, panhandlers, junkies, drug dealers, dog shit, and no green in sight to offset the misery. Sometimes when my Perche neighbours complain that the mayor still hasn't dug that run-off trench he promised, I want to remind them that I saw a man shit in the street five metres from me, while looking at me straight in the eye.

What I don't know is if this sentiment is directly linked to having a country house or is simply the natural trajectory of the white French male, he who moves to the country, grows an abdomen, becomes more conservative, and eventually votes FN. Right now, I fear I'm rounding second.

The other day I found myself once again trolling Mimi Thorisson's site looking for clues and tips about how the house could become more like Winterfell; how I could dress up Bibi and Otto and Anaïs in wolf fur capes maybe and call myself the Warden of the Perche. Halfway down the blog scroll of ceramic bowls of cherries, Cabernet harvests, and a fine collection of wall-hanging copper pots, I realised I'd become that French gentleman farmer I wanted to be, just not in the way I envisioned it.

And as the days have bled into months that have haemorrhaged now into years, I've proven to myself time and time again, with my by-the-seat-of-my-pants home repairs, fraudulent insurance claims, bounced cheques, or playing baseball with all our rotten apples, my goal has never been to become a wholesome Burberry ad like Mimi, nor to spend a charming picturesque year like Peter Mayle, but to create my own modest *maison de famille*, which I'll probably never sell (because nobody will ever buy it), and which I now only look forward to dropping into the laps of my children, who themselves will gripe over it for the many decades to come.

It is they who will bitch about who should fix the roof and who gets to *use it for free*, what circuitous route they should take back to Paris, who pays the heating bill, and what to do with all the Matt Damon DVDs Dad bought at some *vide-grenier*. While, all this time, John (because we're using the third person now) will be out back in the family plot underground, buried with the proceeds he won from Peter Mayle's publishers, enjoying, year after year after year, his own eternal assimilation into French *terroir*.

CHAPTER ELEVEN

THE FRENCH RESISTANT

I'VE MET ALL KINDS OF FRENCH PEOPLE and the one trait they share is that everyone – and I mean everyone – claims to have had a French resistant in the family in World War II. It's either a grandfather or great-uncle – a hero who risked life and limb to do what was *'juste'*. I sometimes have my doubts, given France's dubious wartime history: the quick capitulation, the collaborator Vichy government, not to mention the treatment of French Jews. But when someone's across from you bragging about their family past, it's tough to stop them mid-sentence to clarify: 'Wait a minute, are we talking about the same war?' No, I'm inclined to take their word for it. Plus, the idea of resistance and revolution and standing up for one's rights is something I always admire in the French, something I hoped would rub off on me, once I made France my home.

Before moving here, I'd been pretty much apolitical. I was a young adult during the Clinton years, an era I associate more with short shorts and Arsenio Hall than political engagement. Politics to me was the Lewinsky scandal, and current events were John Wayne Bobbitt – basically bad TV compared to today's really good reality TV. Whereas now, of course, I know all of Trump's hires and fires and can recite to you every Obama legacy he's tried to torpedo.

In this, I've perhaps been led by France, a country that, it seemed, has always cared about politics. It is a place where farmers burn tyres on the motorways to fight for agricultural subsidies, and where an ex-farmer like José Bové can ransack a McDonald's and turn it into a political career. These people don't wait for the political process 'to play out'. They take their future into their own hands, literally. Noël Godin, a self-proclaimed 'humourist-anarchist', went so far as to toss pies in the faces of politicians, lying in wait at a press conference or outside a cabinet meeting, then *entarter* an unsuspecting target à la Buster Keaton. Back in the States, when I lived there, nobody threw a pie in Newt Gingrich's face. And come to think of it, why the hell not?

My time in France got off to a politically charged start when, the day after our wedding, Anaïs and I woke up to a hideous hangover. Jean-Marie Le Pen, the extreme right-wing leader of the National Front party, had made it through the first round of the 2002 presidential primaries, scoring a run-off against the incumbent, Jacques Chirac. For our friends, this was an out of nowhere, seismic event. Lionel Jospin, who'd been favoured to win it all, had come in third and was now eliminated. Jospin had been such a shoo-in, many on the left and centre hadn't even bothered to vote (they were at our wedding instead), or they'd voted for a candidate who had no chance of winning as a way to send Jospin a message moving into the second round.

Jospin was Al Gore's French twin, a number two who was as effective as he was uncharismatic. The problem was that voters liked him – they just didn't love him. And, since his stint as prime minister had been fairly drama-free, voters expected the same on Election Day.

Within hours of the result, most of France took to the streets in a call to arms to ward off a potential Le Pen presidency. Anaïs was too pregnant to join that day, so we stayed at home and watched on TV, amazed at the crowds gathering at the Place de la République and on the Champ de Mars near the Eiffel Tower, marching like a modern day *Les Misérables,* all without (imagine this) the help of social media. Although they detested Chirac, those on the left swallowed their pride and gave him their vote, creating what was called a *barrage républicain* (a Republican firewall). And it worked! Le Pen was trounced in the general election two weeks later, 82 to 18 per cent.

Little did I know, that feel-good moment of May 2002 not only glossed over the underlying problems that had led to this Le Pen insurgency, it also ushered in a pointless five-year second term that would challenge Boris Yeltsin's for doddering nothingness. The economy stalled, morale plunged, and the political torpor I watched ensue would define French politics for the next fifteen years.

During those early months, though, I lived like an undergrad hopped up on Robespierre and Marx, intrigued at this France and its fired-up notion of *citoyenneté.* This was a country with a thirty-five-hour work week, for crying out loud, a civilised luxury earned – I was sure – by the blood of strikers and radicals. There was also the law that banned shopping on Sundays, proving France felt people who worked in department stores had lives, too. Neither of these laws could have flown in the States, but here they were gospel. I imagined the French employee as someone both proud and protected, and the workplace as a teeming cauldron of vigilance, where bosses dared not stretch the day one minute longer, lest they be strung up on the nearest lamppost. An American could learn from these French, I thought. There was a never-satisfied anger inside them I wanted a part of, and within days of moving into our new apartment, I found myself bellied up to the zinc bar of my local café hoping to somehow get a taste.

Next to me stood a ragtag bunch: street sweepers, hipster dads, and a motley group of retirees, men and women, all watching the morning political roundup on the TV behind the bar. You can imagine my excitement when *'ils sont tous des escrocs!'* (they're all crooks), then *'rien ne change!'* (nothing changes!), then *'que de la merde!'* (all of it . . . shit!) rang out from one onlooker after another, building in a violent crescendo. I silently sipped my espresso half expecting this rage to pour out onto the street, where we'd all turn over a car or torch a scooter. But no. At the commercial break, everyone downed their *petit blanc* and folded their newspapers and went out for a smoke, leaving me alone at the bar wondering if I should punch someone.

I knew coming here that it was a French habit to criticise things and say everything was *de la merde*. But I assumed it was with verve and for a noble cause born from a 'the world will hear my voice!' passion. Yet the more I visited this café and frequented offices and dinner parties and school outings, the more I sensed a feeling of disenchantment and disillusionment, something I would have attributed to my bong-smoking American dorm-mates in college, not the descendants of Rousseau. Many felt that the recent war in Iraq had done incredible damage. Not only did many feel lied to, there was a darker feeling that, despite protests and the warnings and fears, the war had happened anyway; their voices and thoughts didn't count.

If you lingered long enough at my bar, these people would eventually get around to the good old days, specifically *les trente glorieuses* (the thirty glorious years), a boom period for the French middle class, one that stretched from the end of World War II until *le choc pétrolier* (the oil crisis of the seventies). I'd heard of these *trente glorieuses* before, but I'd always assumed it defined a group of leaders like 'the dirty dozen', not an actual period of time. For my bar-mates, though, *les trente glorieuses* was a high-water mark for France, and one that had unfortunately begotten *les trente années de crise*, three decades of economic recession and weak-kneed governance. Blame was thrown around, sure, but often it was placed at the feet of French politicians, whom my friends didn't see as revered statesmen, but instead as needy egomaniacs. And the TV I watched in those early years confirmed this.

One popular programme, *Le Grand Journal*, would invite elected officials on, only to make fun of them to their face. The set-up was always the same. A comedian would sit directly across from the guest, then launch into a not-so-nice takedown bio starting with something like 'You're elected mayor of Lyon as a left-leaning candidate in 1993. Two marriages and a bankrupt city later, you resurface on the national scene as a candidate of the right.' It was borderline S&M TV, and yet politicians kept coming back for more, probably because they saw how the audience pitied them. Jacques Chirac capitalised on this sympathy thanks to the *Les Guignols* (*News Puppets*), a satire series featuring marionette versions of real-life politicians. Nearing the end of Chirac's first term, *Les Guignols* portrayed him as a dementia-ridden mess, shuffling around in his slippers, hands in his pockets, whimpering to his wife, Bernadette, 'Nobody likes me, dear. Nobody wants to play with me any more.' Chirac's popularity received an unexpected bump from the episodes, leading some to say the marionette version of Jacques Chirac did more for Jacques Chirac in 2002 than Jacques Chirac himself.

The more I watched, the more I realised what those in my café were pissed off about. The political talent pool was super-shallow. Some officials resembled villains from *Austin Powers* movies more than real candidates. There was Jean-Marie Le Pen, of course, who was rumoured to have tortured captives during the Algerian War and once even wore an eyepatch. There was Bernard Tapie, a former cabinet minister and businessman who was found guilty of fixing a match for the Olympique de Marseilles soccer team. And Dominique Strauss-Kahn (DSK), the former socialist candidate and IMF head who was charged with sexual assault in New York, and who shouldn't be confused with Dominique Bodis, the mayor of Toulouse, who'd been accused (then later exonerated) of attending masked orgies.

None of these guys had written their political obituaries, by the way, as in French politics there's a sort of 'once you're in, you're in' lifer mentality. We may think 'career politician' was an American invention, but the French made it an art form. For every John Edwards, Michael Dukakis or Dan Quayle, men who've since disappeared into the dustbin of historical losers, there was a Laurent Fabius or Jean-François Copé or Nathalie Kosciusko-Morizet, who, despite loss after loss, cabinet appointment after cabinet resignation, were proof that French politicians never die, they just create a hellish political *Groundhog Day* instead.

There were also the terms themselves. Up until 2000, a French presidential term was seven years (it became five years). François Mitterrand served two seven-year terms. His presidency was longer than FDR's. There was a point at which my sister-in-law had lived under only three French presidents, and she was already thirty! And during those *quinquennats* (they even sound ancient), the feeling was that nothing consequential would change. Each campaign would highlight the old issues of jobs going overseas or wages stagnating or the national debt rising, but once the candidate was elected, inertia would again take hold. And the result? Voter turnout dropped every year.

But, for an American, the real cause behind this apathy wasn't the candidates themselves or their long terms in office, but the lack of political difference among voters. France is a pro-abortion, anti-death penalty, pro-gun-control country that's 100 per cent for single-payer health-care coverage. Whereas in America those issues might be contentious, there's national consensus in France. And as a result, political debates usually focus on whether the retirement age should be pushed to sixty-five rather than sixty-two or whether the education budget should be lowered or what role France should play in Europe. During debates, I'd watch dumbfounded, amazed at how eloquently each candidate explained his or her position, wondering when one would challenge the other to see if he had the guts to snuff Bin Laden. But it never came. Of course, the French were disenchanted with the process. It was too boring.

As for all the protests I assumed I'd be participating in each week, they were few and far between. And, if we were marching, it was usually against something the United States had done, whether its involvement in Iraq or against some American-financed genetically modified weedkiller that the EU was flirting with allowing into the country. Although I never questioned such stances, it did feel weird to shit on my country from abroad. It was like playing political dress-up, John promenading down Boulevard Saint-Germain with his cardboard *'Non à la guerre'* poster, ducking into cafés to grab an espresso and pee, not having to worry if he'd be water cannoned or arrested.

The only French person it seemed who hadn't lost faith in the politics of change was my wife. Anaïs was a *socialiste militante*, meaning she was a card-carrying member of the Socialist Party, not just a regular run-of-the-mill socialist voter. In Eastern Bloc countries in the 1970s she might have been that person who locked you up, but in France a *militant* was more organiser than *subcommandante*. Anaïs attended party events, voted on its direction and platform, and generally kept abreast of the issues and how the party was addressing them. When we first arrived in France, I took her once-a-month 'I'm off to my *meeting*' departures from the house as proof she was a recovering alcoholic, something she'd apparently been hiding from me before we got married. It wasn't until later, when I found out 'meeting' meant *socialist rally*, that I started to worry.

Most of our friends now know Anaïs is an actual *militante*. As many our age have drifted toward the centre, as all sell-outs do, Anaïs continues to swim upstream, refusing to concede that public services need to be cut or that the unions are full of opportunists. For many bourgeois French, voting socialist is something they feel they should do, but don't love doing. And none of them head off to a monthly meeting on a February weeknight to cheer everyone on.

Anaïs walks the walk. When we receive our annual tax bill, I can feel her disappointment. 'That's it? That's all?' she'll say as I shudder in the corner as if stricken with polio.

'You just say that because you can vote,' I tell her, bringing up a sore subject for us, one which I remind her of every election cycle when I stay at home and brood while the rest of France decides my future for me. As the years pass, it becomes more and more infuriating to be unable to vote in this country, especially one with such a high abstention rate. I often think of proposing a vote 'proxy' idea, where foreigners can vote in place of the lazy apathetic French who'd rather play Xbox. Anaïs sympathised, to a point: 'Well, get off your ass and become French, then,' was her usual response, which I always found a bit of a blunt solution.

She knew it stung, especially considering I vote overseas as a Democrat from the state of New York, a vote about as worthless as a candy wrapper. But Anaïs believes all movements start with one vote, and when our French friends tell us they didn't have time to vote in a certain election, whether it be municipal or European or parliamentary, I can see her seethe. Anaïs cares, maybe too much. Once I came home to find her draped over the radio crying, looking like someone in the forties who'd just received news about Pearl Harbor. I assumed the worst, only to find out it was just the announcement of the cabinet for the recently elected president, Nicolas Sarkozy.

Seeing I had no skin in the game, Sarkozy, to me, was a blast. He was a weird Eurotrash version of a bad American president. He had billionaire friends and didn't apologise about it. He went for jogs in his FDNY T-shirt and Yankees hat. He had no qualms screwing over his right-wing constituents, and there was always an angry scowl to him as if becoming president was a score he settled with those who bullied him at school. 'Sarko' was kind of a test run for a new mould of French president, one more rough and populist on the edges. He didn't have the *grande école* pedigree his predecessors had, and he once told a heckler to *'Casse-toi pauvre con'* ('Get the fuck out of my face, you loser'), which wasn't a phrase you'd hear from the Mitterands or Pompidous. He separated from his wife, Cecilia, the day he was elected president and then shacked up months later with Carla Bruni, a model/singer who'd once dated Mick Jagger. The best thing about Sarko was that his goal of *Thatcherising* France, urging it to *'travailler plus pour gagner plus'* ('Work more to earn more'), blew up in his face and forced France back into the streets, inflaming a latent anger.

Under Sarko, unrest was palpable. We had our bad guy, but just when it seemed as if France was getting its resistance mojo back and giving me some political direction, Obama was elected, plunging France once again back into its Lyme-diseased apathy. All of a sudden, the United States was no longer a neocon warmongering crooked sub-prime-banking foothold to protest. It was Kennedy-esque and forward-thinking, and when my friends saw clips of Obama at the White House Correspondents' dinner and compared him to the stiffs France continued to turn out, they could only offer *'bah. . . . oui'* sighs. 'Of course you have Obama as president. You're constantly changing,' my friend Nicolas told me. 'We still have a feudal system in place. We never change.'

But France was changing, slowly, and the one who benefited the most from the Mitterrand/Chirac/Sarkozy sloth was Marine Le Pen, Jean-Marie's daughter, who'd gradually climbed in the polls since taking over the FN from her father in 2011. Weirdly, Marine Le Pen's message, aside from dittoing her father's xenophobia and populist nationalism and hatred for Europe, also homed in on what those in my café had voiced to me in those early years: France needed to break with the same old heads, but in a robust way.

Listening to Le Pen and her supporters, it felt as if I'd been following a conversation that wasn't at all what I thought it was. Those who felt disgusted and fed up weren't at all apathetic, I realised. They were revolutionary and angry, charged with a 'pull down the circus tent' self-destruction that hadn't reared its head since 1914, when the entire continent committed suicide, or in the Vichy days, when France sold its soul. In 2016, as President François Hollande's popularity dropped and Le Pen rallies grew larger and larger, I feared for the French and this place I knew as home, not knowing it would be my own country shooting itself in the foot come November.

Following Trump's victory and during the months leading up to the French presidential election in May, I suffered a sort of election PTSD. The impossible was now possible. Yet nobody seemed to care.

'I don't think you understand. She's going to fucking win!' I found myself shrieking at friends, killing any enjoyment to be had at the dinner table. For me, Marine Le Pen was the third part of the apocalypse puzzle falling into place; the one that started with Brexit and was followed by Trump, which would eventually start the process of the dissolution of Europe, the end of NATO, the death of the euro and John's abdicating his right to a sound sleep.

Up until now, and despite its lame politics and general inertia, I still found France quirky and classy, kind of like the older woman you cross on the ground floor of your building, who is still chic despite the fact she hasn't paid her common charges in years. With Le Pen, this older lady became something darker, inhabited by a growing spectre who'd been haunting me since my arrival. Not only did Dad ruin my honeymoon, daughter had slowly weaselled her way into my daily life, constantly yapping on the radio and talk show circuit, harping on about her fetish issues of immigration and Europe, two subjects that she knew she could use to divide France. Like Trump's, her base came largely from two areas – the disenfranchised industrial north, where industry was in decline, and the south, where the FN had been formed in the early 1970s by ex-Algerian Pieds Noirs, settlers who'd felt betrayed by Charles de Gaulle's decision to pull France out of Algeria.

The common refrain in the media was that the FN follower was 'Make America Great Again' *à la Française* – a voter suffering from his or her job moving overseas and the notion that his or her old way of French life had been abandoned by the culturally diverse France of today. But that didn't tell the whole story. There were affluent FN supporters, many in the south of France, who were simply happy to find their racism echoed on a national scale. Where Le Pen differed from Trump, though, was that nobody underestimated her ability as a candidate.

She wasn't the bombastic glass-eyed blowhard her father was. She was a lawyer, feared as an adversary, and with an ability to turn an argument upside down in her favour with an oozing grin. She was also shameless, taking time out of her spring 2017 campaign to visit Trump Tower and look as if she was having meetings with the president-elect, when in fact she was just riding up and down the escalator.

Not only did the extreme right now have their voice, so did the far left, in the form of Jean-Luc Mélenchon, a crusty political dinosaur who'd refashioned himself as 'le French Bernie Sanders.' Compared to Mélenchon, though, Sanders was Mitt Romney. Mélenchon advocated stuff even the French socialists found out there, including a 100 per cent tax on top level income and a new axis of allies that included the true democracies of Russia and Venezuela.

Mélenchon lived in the Tenth. We shared the same café in the morning, and I'd see him sometimes, huddling with his younger staff in the corner, with a grizzled look, as if he'd just swallowed laundry soap. He was a gruff interview and great orator, adored on the left for zinging the right and loved on the right for torpedoing those on the left that he called *gauche caviar,* the French equivalent of 'Champagne Socialist' (Champagne being pretty much classless in France). What nobody knew was that Mélenchon actually thought he could win. And, while everyone cheered on his takedowns and laughed at his quips, he gradually climbed the polls, growing a predominantly youth-based party called *La France Insoumise* (Unbowed France). The possibility of a Le Pen/Mélenchon run-off in the second round was becoming real. And what scared me was that, when faced with the choice of France being a borderline Maoist country or a

Fascist one, centrist voters might choose to stay home, clearing a Le Pen path to victory.

The campaign had also been rocked by something that usually doesn't happen in French politics. Hollande, the presiding president, channelled his inner LBJ and chose not to seek a second term, something that hadn't been done since the Fifth Republic was formed. Hollande's own party had abandoned him for his pandering to the right, and the economic programmes he'd implemented had begun bearing fruit much too late to stop his downward spiral. It also seemed he hated the job. His suits never really fitted. He'd put on weight. He'd cheated on his girlfriend, the journalist Valérie Trierweiler, with the actress Julie Gayet, and was paid back in full when Trierweiler published a tell-all that became a bestseller. To his credit, Hollande never milked the Paris terrorist attacks as other cynical presidents might have done. He was steady and solemn, appearing at the site of the massacre at the Bataclan the night of the shooting to grieve with strangers, ignoring security risks. He did what leaders rarely do on those occasions – not make it about them. He was, to my mind, funny and insanely intelligent, and completely unfit for the job. But when I suggested to friends that maybe his most deft political move was to drop out at the right time to help prevent a Le Pen victory, this was met with disdain. 'He's bowing out because he sucks,' one said. 'He should have bowed out when he was born.'

Nonetheless, Hollande's decision to retire made him look downright saintly compared to François Fillon, the centre-right candidate and early favourite who'd become enmeshed in a scandal when it was revealed his wife and children had been receiving salaries as his parliamentary staff, despite never working for him. His downfall was one of many October surprises that made this French campaign feel downright American.

The only thing that helped me keep faith was the first-round debate, a four-hour round robin featuring all thirteen candidates. All on network TV, in prime time. The star of the show was an ex-factory worker called Philippe Poutou, who represented the *Nouveau Parti Anticapitaliste* (*NPA*) and who wore a long-sleeved T-shirt as an upgrade on his usual white tank top. Next to him stood Nathalie Arthaud from the *Lutte Ouvrière* (Workers' Struggle), offering strident screams about offshore accounts and bank graft, and Jean Lassalle, whose six-foot-eight frame and heavy Basque-accented French gave him the air of a Spanish Lurch from *The Addams Family*. This was democracy, I told myself. Everybody had their say, and French voters could now go to sleep, knowing they'd never vote for any of them.

After the first round of votes, the two candidates left standing were Marine Le Pen and Emmanuel Macron. Le Pen I'd expected, but not Macron. During the debates, he seemed too reserved to be formidable, too young to be credible, and too *bougie* to carry any weight in rural France. Macron was everyone's second choice, like Hillary Clinton in the Democratic primaries. But in France, everyone's second choice is where you want to be as a candidate.

All I'd known about Macron was that he came from the *grandes écoles* and had worked in banking before serving under Hollande as economic minister, and then shrewdly departing the sinking ship. Oh, and that his wife was a lot older than he was. But, in line with the French tradition of not prying into the private lives of candidates, his unusual marriage was never an issue. What was the issue was whether Mélenchon's people would vote for Macron. Many of the *insoumises* were acting like pissed-off adolescents, claiming they couldn't vote for Macron, as 'there's no real difference between the two'. For them, ruled by a fascist or an ex-banker were the same. Mélanchon himself remained strangely coy when asked if he'd support Macron. His reply, 'I'll leave it up to my followers to decide for themselves,' felt like an enormous (and dangerous) dodge. Adding to my fear were the Fillon voters, who were bitter their candidate's rightful path to the throne had been blocked by a vengeful press. Macron was Hollande II to them and, considering how unpopular Hollande was, Le Pen couldn't do worse.

Amidst all this noise, I wasn't convinced the French would hold their Republican wall like they had in 2002. Too much seemed fractured now. Too many promises had been broken by previous administrations. This country, which I'd so admired before, was just as petty and craven as America and going down the tubes right along with us.

What I never could have predicted was that the election may have been decided by something France doesn't have and America has too much of – cable news. According to French law, all campaigning and media coverage must cease forty-eight hours *before* the polls open. It's designed to create a cool-down period during which James Comey letters and million-dollar thirty-second spots can't convince people to vote against their own interests.

Apparently nobody on the Russia hacker side received this memo, though, and during the press blackout a dump of thousands of emails from Macron's computer flooded the Internet with, of course, rumours of offshore accounts and shady financial dealings, none of which could be verified or debunked in time. But there was no network like Fox News cynical enough to pick up the story. Le Pen tried to comment but couldn't. And during the forty-eight hours, instead of a Julian Assange October surprise dominating French dinners and conversations, 'Macron leaks' festered and collapsed under their now-nothing weight.

Another campaign law states that networks cannot broadcast exit polls or overseas ballot results before voting polls close. Instead, the result for every French presidential election is announced on the dot at 8pm on the second Sunday in May, in countdown fashion, with the next winner's face appearing on your screen in a 3 ... 2 ... 1 ta-da! fashion.

Because of this, election night for me was like a horrifying New Year's Eve celebration. 'Three minutes, people. We have three minutes left!' I yelled as I ran around the living room, holding a throw pillow like a football. And as the seconds ticked down, I felt like a man whose time in France had just run out. I saw my visa expiring and us having to move back to the States. I saw Otto's friends in the neighbourhood fearful for their parents' immigration status. And all the ghouls I'd seen on TV would now be in actual positions of power. The snakelike Florian Philippot would be giving daily bullshit presidential press conferences à la Sarah Huckabee Sanders. Marine Le Pen's niece, the twenty-eight-year-old Marion Maréchal-Le Pen, the one who laced her talk with *c'est du délire* ('it's like, crazy'), would probably serve as her Jared Kushner adviser. This is how it happens, I told myself. The small losses pile up, and all of a sudden there's a Trump in every country, like a chain of extreme-right Starbucks.

3 ... 2 ... 1 ...

And then none of that happened. Macron flashed up on the screen with a 65 to 35 per cent split. Le Pen faded into the background. The fever broke. The champagne flowed. And as Le Pen made her concession speech minutes later, I kissed Anaïs and hugged my friends. We'd live.

My French friends were just as happy as I was, but their reaction seemed more muted. 'But of course, we won! We had zem all ze way!'

This lame attempt at American slang was a way I realize to deflect from the awkwardness of them having to take a grown man into their arms like a child who'd just run into their bedroom crying about a nightmare. "Every zing will be all right, John.' (The wicked witch is dead.). So French. I could have killed them right there.

These lucky bastards, I thought. For all their griping about the political process these past years, the French, in the end, found their true north. Mélenchon's *unsubmissives* dragged their asses to the polls just like all the penny-loafered *Fillonistes* did, both whining all the way to the ballot boxes, but voting regardless, adding their own bitter brick to the Republican wall. Perhaps Susan Sarandon could have learned from them, I thought, or Jill Stein, or those suburban moms who'd once voted for Obama and now Trump. True democracy, the French were teaching me, involves swallowing loads of shit to arrive at a consensual second choice we could now all critique.

Months later, I'd watch as the pendulum of public opinion swung the opposite way, as for a time Macron looked like a French Kennedy or at least a Justin Trudeau.

And as I combed through all the American texts and emails that flooded my phone and computer, I sensed jealousy and admiration for my French compatriots, those whom I had originally admired, then written off, and now found heroic. In a way, Marine Le Pen had given me what I'd been searching for since arriving in France – an appreciation of French resolve and a commitment to be an engaged citizen, a promise I made to myself during that 3 ... 2 ... 1 countdown.

Now I hand out coffee to the refugees on some mornings with Anaïs. I know the mayor of the Tenth by name, and I've even found an email address of someone on his staff, whom I now bomb with photos of all the garbage sitting on our street.

And don't worry. Macron was soon in Anaïs's crosshairs. 'What?' she told me, after Macron announced changes he planned to implement in the labour law. 'I'm supposed to give him a pass simply because he's not Le Pen? Fuck him! Oh, and you want to know what? His English, which he thinks is really good? It actually sucks.'

That was true enough. And Macron's popularity, which for a time had the French press dubbing him not just a French Obama, but a 'French Jupiter', a young leader who could have his Napoleonic way with France, was not to last. He was intent on reforming – and the French don't take reforms sitting down, especially if they look like setting the Republic on a path to becoming American. And that, to my mind, was how it was all set to go: shopping on Sundays with credit cards, fewer public services (meaning late trains, expensive schooling and long waits at the hospital) and people working multiple jobs. For Macron, and some French, these may seem like necessary steps to be competitive. But to others, the idea that it's normal to work until seventy-five or normal to have private health insurance sucks. And, for people like me, it's a total nightmare. Because the goal of every American expat, I've learned, is to live a normally modest European life, which we secretly know (but don't tell anyone) is a rich American life.

While I was writing this book, Macron began facing his first true test in the form of the *Gilets Jaunes* (Yellow Vests), a national wave of protesters who seeped up through the floorboards to not only imperil many of the reforms he wanted to implement, but also his government and maybe even his presidency. For a succession of weekends, protesters wearing the fluorescent-coloured safety vests (required of all French drivers to keep in their cars in case of an accident or breakdown) descended on Paris without any union affiliation or organisation and no real leader and wreaked havoc on the Champs-Élysées. They were initially protesting the fuel tax that Macron's government inserted into the 2019 budget to help France meet Paris climate accord standards. But that tax was just the tip of the iceberg for a swathe of the population who feel France's working class was paying a bill that France's one per cent or French corporations should be picking up.

Macron caved to their demands, suspending the ecofuel tax for 2019, while also raising the French minimum wage by €100 a month. But by the year end the focus was on pension reforms, the trains had ground to a halt, and half the country was taking industrial action, while the von Sothens were taking to their bikes.

During my morning café chats nowadays, I'm often asked by those at the bar when the United States will have its own *Gilets Jaunes* moment. 'When will Americans rise up and say *non!* John?' And the excuses I usually give, like 'Americans just don't protest like that' or 'We no longer have the unions like you guys do' or 'Well, if you go on strike, you lose your health care, you see,' strike me as a bit half-assed. Usually our TV above the bar is flashing something nightmarish that happened in the States the day before, and often it's me who's doing the *que de la merde!* My resentment doesn't come just from the daily barrage of the American president, separating immigrant children from their parents, but from the numbing acceptance by all of us in the supposed 'resistance'. The ones who told me they'd move to Canada or France if Trump was elected, but who send five Facebook posts per day instead.

And, while I sit here holding my espresso, hemming and hawing, I realise I'm not much different. I've done little more than the other guys. And that's how revisionism works, folks. Everyone's a resistant, everyone is *juste* – until they aren't. Personally, I can't stomach the thought of my descendants one day bragging to their friends how their great-grandfather John, although American, was a French resistant. That, just like the French during the American Revolution, he joined the good side during the dark times in America by courageously making podcasts and donating to Shareblue Media and retweeting Keith Olbermann videos, all from his apartment in the Tenth, right off of the north-south artery, ironically named Rue Lafayette.

No. The one thing I've learned from my French confrères and my militant wife and Dumpster-burning daughter is that if you're going to say *non!* you better be willing to be *non!*

Hold my beer, *mes amis*. I'm off to bake some pies.

CHAPTER TWELVE

NO PLACE LIKE
CHEZ MOI

SOME OF THE MOST VIVID MEMORIES I have of my parents are of their cocktail parties. They hosted so often, it was odd if a Friday night passed and there weren't adults at our door smiling and smelling of perfume. Since these affairs were *chez nous,* there was no need for a babysitter. Nor was I asked to go to my room. Instead, I was expected to dress up and mingle and 'contribute', as my mother said. I didn't mind. I liked it, actually – greeting guests and taking coats, weaving my way through all the people who seemed, at the time, taller than trees.

'Well, get a load of this one!' someone would say. 'That's Johnny von Sothen! One of the all-time all-timers!' A heavy paw would land on my shoulder or someone would rub the top of my head. These voices were smoky and loud, but never threatening. 'You may not remember me, dear, but the last time I saw you, you were this high!' I'd turn to find an older woman with pearls and dead vocal cords marking a point around her shin. 'And already you were working for

Kissinger!' Everyone would roar, and I'd smile and laugh, although unsure why.

On occasion, I'd sit at the table and eat with these adults, observing how they talked, mimicking how they held their forks, noticing how their speech grew louder as they belted back more wine. It was there I learned that at a party you could talk about something horribly boring to someone and they'd still make an effort to listen.

'Well, Nick Tucker took my notebook this week,' I'd tell my neighbour, Sylvia Ward. 'And he ripped out the pages that had my geography assignment inside. And Sally Myers. She just watched.'

'My land,' Sylvia Ward would fake gasp. 'Well, isn't that a shame?'

'It is, isn't it?' I'd nod, feeling better already.

After dinner the crowd would gather in the living room for a 'nightcap' and my father would play the piano and my mother would sing Fats Waller or Cole Porter. Sometimes they'd hand out sheet music with lyrics, but everyone knew the songs already. I didn't, though, so I'd sit on the stairs and listen. And that was okay, too. I didn't feel alone or odd at the moment, just someone watching a world not mine, one with its own rules and language.

When the party ended, if I was still awake, I'd take part in the autopsy of the night with my parents while they cleaned up. We'd discuss who'd impressed and who was a bore. I'd imitate a guest with an adult-sounding voice or make fun of someone, imitating my father's style. 'Jeez, Mr Langford,' I'd start. 'When that guy comes into a room, it's like someone just left.' They'd laugh and I'd feel as if I'd *contributed*, even if I had no idea what I just said.

These situations and these moments would forever hold allure for me, especially when I moved to France, because, I realise now, the life of an *étranger* is much like being the only child of older parents who hold tons of cocktail parties. You're embarrassed for being there and it's obvious you stand out. You're treated (often) like a child. You don't know the formal codes and you're learning on the fly. Since you assume people are feigning interest in you, you pick up tics and quick-witted dodges to make yourself more endearing or to better hide your deficiencies. And in the end, you go to your room exhausted, not really sure if you had a good time, not really sure why you were there in the first place, but content nonetheless.

This feeling of being on the periphery drives many people nuts. Most need to be sure they understand everything or know everyone or at least grasp why it is they've been invited. Anything outside that realm can seem spooky. Not for me. Talking about stuff I didn't understand, navigating weird rules, feeling alone but safe, the daily life of an expat basically, never seemed daunting. It was home, actually, something I'd been born for.

🕎 🕎 🕎

When people cite the reason they choose to live abroad, the emphasis is usually on the pull part – what drew them to the place. It could be that job. It could be a love interest, maybe a passion for eighteenth-century painting, but rarely do they talk about the fleeing part – what made them bail. And this is odd, considering that the chance to leave is probably the real reason they're living abroad.

People think I moved to France for *l'amour,* and that's the version I usually provide, because it fits a nice story arc. But there were other contributing factors, namely my mother and my father.

Although my parents lived in Georgetown and I lived in New York, I often felt I still lived with them. We'd talk twice a day usually, both of them on the phone at the same time, one upstairs and one in the kitchen. And, if you heard their excited voices, you'd think I'd just been released from a Burmese jail. My call was the highlight of their day.

'Okay, I'm on!' Dad would yell into the receiver. 'What did I miss?' The fact we'd spoken that morning was one he'd already forgotten.

'Well, I was about to say . . .' My mother would then start in, using the call as a chance to give me unsolicited career advice. 'John should try to get a real estate broker's licence.' The fact I'd just told her I'd had a piece published hadn't registered. Nothing could. Their lives on the other end sounded chaotic. Fox News was blaring. The dog was barking. The TV had taken over a large part of their day at this point, and in its wake lay the dinners with friends at the club, or trips to the pool or weeks down at Cape Hatteras. My mother had been diagnosed with MS and my father with Parkinson's and, although they still lived in the same brownstone in Georgetown, their movement was limited to the bedroom upstairs and the family room downstairs in the back of the house where the kitchen and the Rush Limbaugh show lurked. The rest of the house sat like an exquisite antechamber at Versailles – meticulous and un-used. The dining room, my father said, 'you could cordon off with a velvet rope.'

Both seemed to maintain a sense of humour about their predicament. Parkinson's to Dad was 'some dopey thing, I don't know'. Mom chalked up her limping and fatigue to arthritis and, since it was just aches and pains, she just gobbled Advil and walked with a cane. A wheelchair, to her, 'looked sickly'. The reason we spoke so much, though, was that I was usually following up on a neighbour's call I'd received the previous night telling me they'd heard Mom fall down the stairs or that my father looked disoriented at the Safeway yesterday, his pants falling down.

Eventually these calls would become frequent and my trips down to DC multiplied. Soon I was fluent in their prescriptions and I had a calendar alerting me of doctor visits and rehab sessions. I read up on how each disease would progress. There was a stack of powers of attorney forms for me to sign. And during these Amtrak rides or in the late hours of a Saturday night when I'd find a message on my answering machine alerting me to another meltdown, I dreamed of having a sibling, someone I probably hated but who could at least share my mom and dad responsibilities, so I could come back to my NYC apartment, get high and sleep with a semi-stranger in peace.

And when I'd make the trips back to Georgetown, it's not like Mom and Dad seemed happy to see me. 'Why are *you* here?' my mother would ask. She'd, of course, downplay whatever the neighbour had told me with an 'Oh, we're fine,' and since that was exactly what I wanted to hear, I'd take her word for it and head back up to New York, using age as my convenient out. For the career advice I could tell myself, 'They're old! What do they know?' And, for the health fears, 'They're old, they know themselves better than anyone else!'

Ever since I was a child, I'd defined my parents by their age. They stood out from the others. In grade school, I was embarrassed when someone in my class asked why my grandfather had shown up for Father's Day. While other dads had either fought in Vietnam or protested Vietnam, my father had fought in World War II. While other houses had The Who or Beatles albums next to the record player, my parents listened to Benny Goodman and Artie Shaw.

There are no photos of my dad with bell-bottoms or my mother with Elton John-type sunglasses. When I found out Josh Byron's parents were getting divorced, I asked if my parents ever planned on doing the same.

'No,' my father replied. 'We're too old.'

And I believed them. They were too old to buy a Porsche or have an affair, too old to drop acid or start a second career. That stuff was for young parents. And as the years passed, I grew to love this about them. All of a sudden, their lifestyle seemed retro to me, and in a way, it mirrored mine. They drank hard liquor still, or 'highballs', as Dad called them. They didn't exercise or watch what they ate. They kept late hours. They had a rotary phone and drove a fake-wood-panelled station wagon. Although I was in my early thirties, they were the same as when I was ten: elder Dorian Grays, frozen in a hard-driving mid-fifties lifestyle, despite being close to eighty. And like them, I'd remained frozen, too.

Becoming a father and a husband had thawed me some, sure. But there remained a part of me that still clung to home, home being where my parents were, of course. Even when Anaïs and I settled in Paris, I assumed our time here would be brief, like a stint in the Peace Corps. We'd do our two or three years, maybe have another kid, take advantage of the free health care and something called an *allocation familiale* (a government stipend paid to you each month by the French government for, I guess, being fertile), then head back to reality, the reality being closer to my parents. What I didn't plan on was the routine we quickly found ourselves liking, and work coming easier than I expected. Soon we were 'acclimated', as expats say, and considering staying on.

This isn't to say I wasn't in the States a lot. I was. Every two months or so, I'd find myself on an Air France flight just like those Amtrak trains. Granted, the situation with Mom and Dad had to be a bit dire for me to go, but travel wasn't out of the ordinary. And after each trip, I'd return to France content in knowing I'd defused yet another emergency, only to find out my mother would scuttle those plans within the week.

'I let that nurse you hired go. We didn't need her.'

'No need for that staircase elevator you wanted installed. Too expensive. We'll manage.'

'We're thinking of heading down to Florida next week. Don't worry, I'll drive.'

Don't worry. We'll manage. All good. We're fine. Words were one thing, their actions another. I know they didn't mean to sabotage their life to keep me close, but that was the result. I could never fully commit to my life in France. Everything in America seemed pressing and life threatening, while things back home in Paris felt trivial or dilettantish. Suddenly a meeting with a magazine editor for a small piece about a restaurant opening could be blown off, because, well, I was flying out the next day. Feeding Bibi with a spoon her first year should have been magical, but instead it reminded me of my father wearing a bib at dinner. I lived in two homes an ocean apart, spread between two families.

As the doctors predicted, Mom's and Dad's conditions worsened, and soon it became obvious they needed assisted care. We sold their house and held a giant yard sale a month before the signing, with friends and neighbours flocking to buy four floors of stuff. I didn't realise it at the time, but

Mom's idea to invite everyone was her way of saying good-bye. It was as if all the trappings that had made up those famous cocktail parties were her small organ donations, things that would live on in others long after she was gone.

People picked and schmoozed and many walked out of the house with paintings or sculptures under their arms, my mother waving and smiling, keeping up appearances despite the obvious bittersweet pain. Many of these buyers had been her subjects. There was a painting of two boys constructing a fort in the alley and one of Mr Longfellow in a dentist chair. There was even an eight-foot canvas of a construction site down the block, a wrecking ball tearing through mortar. Mom had a long, prolific career as a painter, starting in Paris, of course, and ending on that day she said goodbye to those works and to her friends. Some of her pieces are in permanent collections in DC, but most are with the people she knew. And she liked it that way. 'Art is food you share,' she told me as she counted the money she'd made that day. Mom liked to sell, too.

Much of how my mother and father met and what they'd built together hit me as I met with the sales agent that month to discuss price and if I needed to be there at closing, since I had the power of attorney, but lived in France. It was brutal selling my childhood home, but I told myself it was necessary. Mom and Dad were facing facts and downsizing their life, and that was a good thing. They might even blossom in their new surroundings, I thought. And perhaps I could finally commit to living in Paris, apart and far from them.

Mom didn't last a year.

We'd organised a trip to Washington that Easter so my parents could meet four-month-old Otto and we could see their new home. Mom, however, developed a nagging cough a week before our departure, and by the time our plane touched down in DC, she was in the hospital with pneumonia.

'Johnnie peaches!' she coughed when she saw me coming through the double doors. I'd rushed from the hotel to the hospital to find her on a stretcher in a hallway. She looked relieved more than happy to see me, as if she had a plan in place, but needed an accomplice to make it work. In minutes, they'd be moving her to the ER.

'Sweetie, take my rings quick.' She handed me everything, even the one with the large sapphire my grandmother had given her. 'I'm dying, you see.'

'Oh, stop. You're not,' I scolded. Everyone had settled in at the hotel room, I told her. And I was still holding the reservation for Easter brunch at the club just in case. 'Oh, and here, Bibi made a drawing for you.' Mom tapped me on the wrist to shoo me for being silly.

'That's great. Now make sure you have my POA and make sure you sign that DNR. No machine for me. Okay?' I didn't like the gallows humour, I told her. It wasn't funny. But within hours she was hooked up to oxygen, and as the days passed and she didn't improve and the doctors told me the antibiotics weren't working, I realised Mom hadn't been bluffing. She was dying.

Eventually she was moved off the ER to her own room, which I took to be progress, but which in reality meant it was all over. They move you so you can die in private with a window and a door, so you don't demoralise all the other patients on the block fighting for their lives. There she was attached to an IV drip with fluids and morphine and I was told I had thirty-six hours to say goodbye to a mother who for all intents and purposes was a healthy, lucid, cancer-free, unsick, not-very-old seventy-five-year-old who'd had a cold last week and was now dying in a bed in front of me.

Weirdly, I thought about the *New York Times* and its series of '36 Hours in...' pieces, which I read religiously in the Sunday editions – '36 Hours in Flagstaff'; '36 Hours in Milan.' Why hadn't anyone written '36 Hours with Your Dying Parent'? It could have helped, I thought – a handy bullet-pointed, must-do listicle with insightful tips. Instead, I found myself winging it. I brought in my father to say goodbye, which would feel a bit tacky if she ended up surviving. A minister from the church came over to pray. My uncle Charlie was brought in, friends as well. The room had a shower, so I didn't leave the hospital, and I slept on a chair next to Mom's bed, waking up every hour to roam the room, watching her breathe. And as the red digital oxygen count on the machine next to her dropped, I'd pick up my pace and talk to Mom faster, realising seventeen, no, sixteen hours were left, give or take. Sometimes I'd go to her left ear and mutter nonsense, then sprint around to the other side of the bed and work the right ear, burrowing into her neck as I'd done as a child when she read me those French books at night in her bed, telling her things I probably shouldn't have shared. Thirteen hours. Twelve hours. I recounted the long road trips we would take down to Cape Hatteras along Route 12, where the sound and the ocean almost touch. The drives where she told me about her old horse Scissors and her red Alpha Romeo, which she drove around Pittsburgh after Vassar, and how Paris meant so much to her. How it had offered her a chance to leave home, as it had for me.

I told Mom how every time I smell turpentine I think of her and those days we spent in her studio, me watching her paint. I brought up all our past dogs: Teddy and Pal and Dr Pepper and Baron. Then there was the raw turkey she cooked on a car engine over Thanksgiving as a way to prep it for the oven in Hatteras. Or the time we found starfish in

the thousands on the beach and she made Christmas orna-
ments out of all of them and how she hosted a sleepover
party for thirty kids on my ninth birthday, then booked
us for the *Bozo's Circus* TV show the next day. For a nine-
year-old to watch himself and his birthday on TV with so
many friends made me feel famous. I told her I was sorry
for staying in Paris, and when her health improved, we'd
take her and Dad back with us and they could get a small
one-bedroom on the Île Saint-Louis maybe. I could be a son
and a husband and a dad now, and she hadn't seen this new
me yet. There was still so much time, so much time, and this
didn't have to be the end.

I brought Otto into the room, and her eyes brightened and
she whispered through her mask that he looked beautiful,
which I took to be a sign she was getting better. 'Otto's magic!'
I thought, 'Otto's saved her!' But the oxygen level continued
to drop, and the hours soon became minutes, and her
breaths became more separated and sparse. And soon a cold
realisation hit me: The time for giving up hope and letting
go was now. It would be my parting gift to her. And as I cried
into Mom's ear and held her hand, and told her it was okay to
let go, that I'd be fine, I felt her chest rise one last time. There
was no long continuous beep like you see in the movies. Just
a deafening silence and my echo of goodbye skipping down
the side of her ear like a coin down a deep well.

There's a part of me that thinks Mom saw her pneumonia as
a way to thread the needle; to die on her own terms without
going through the painful and debilitating next phase that
would have surely seen her even more dependent on me.

Maybe she felt I was old enough now to handle her death, but young enough still to launch a life without her presence dominating it.

Ironically, it's me now who sees friends still locked into perpetual childhoods, unable to escape their parents' judgment or shadow, unable still to chart their own course. In a way, Mom's gift is that, the matriarchal tree dying, so the small poplar behind it could finally grow out from under the shade.

Mom had been giving us signs for a while that her time here was limited. When I told her Anaïs was pregnant with Bibi, her first reaction was, 'Oh. That's wonderful! Now I can die!' I think in a way she'd fought hard the past few years to get me to a point where I could live without her, and once she saw this was possible, the last thing she did as a mother was to show her son how to die with grace.

It was only when I opened up her address book that it hit me she was gone. It was a thick snakeskin thing with professional cards falling out and shopping lists rubber-banded to the back and Post-its on the front jacket. What hurt me wasn't having to call all her old friends and cousins to let them know the news. Instead it was Mom's bad handwriting – not knowing if the 4s were 9s, or who this Mrs Fletcher person was, and realising suddenly she'd never be able to tell me.

It's odd that you're asked to immediately organise things the instant you lose a loved one, things that you have no energy for but that need to be done. Perhaps it's part of our Western culture's mourning process – sandbag someone with immense sorrow and fatigue, then ask them to throw together a funeral, deal with estate issues, and make on-the-dime decisions about cremation, songs and whom to invite. Make it snappy, because Easter vacation's about to end.

Although my suitcase hadn't been opened yet, I was meeting with lawyers, many of whom had questions as to what was left in a trust and what was outside the trust. Who'd be the executor of her estate? Who'd take care of Charlie? Who'd look after Dad? Who, John? Who? I would, I told them. There was nobody else. Of course it would be me. And it's not like I had that much to do in Paris anyway, I thought. It's not like I had a real career or anything. It's just one long Peace Corps stint, right? Nothing that demanding.

Before heading back to Paris, I ate with Dad in the cafeteria of the nursing home and, during our dinner, told him I'd call and that I'd hired a nurse to look after him. An elderly man joined us for coffee. His name was Joe, and just like Dad now, he too was a widower. They'd become friends because both were Washington Senators fans. Joe could see I was pained when I received the text that my cab had arrived. 'We'll be all right, John.' He winked. 'I'll keep this guy on ice.'

I kissed Dad and scrunched his shoulders, then turned to leave to hide my tears, feeling guilty for having expected him to die first. That had been the plan all along. Dad had been the sicker of the two, and it was Mom who'd been taking care of him, dividing his medication in those weekly dispensers, wiping his mouth, keeping his appointments. Every time she'd complain, I'd sympathise and secretly fantasise about life after Dad, where it was just Mom and me and the kids and Anaïs, all of us living in Paris. It would be a way for Mom to reconnect with the life she'd had as a student at Les Beaux-Arts, I told myself, and a chance for me, obviously, to have her back with me. Instead I was in a cab. Mom was gone. And Dad was sitting in a cafeteria with a stranger.

When school reconvened in late April, I dropped the kids off only to bump into my friend Emily, a fellow parent and neighbour. 'So?' she asked innocently. 'How was *vacances*? How were *les States*?' (The French often call the United States '*les States*' now. It's annoying.) I told her what had happened, and regret immediately flashed on her face. But how could she have known? How could anyone know these things?

Following our return, I drifted through Paris in form only, constantly checking in with staff at the facility and planning next steps for Dad's care, considering he'd eventually need more of it. Everything that should have made me like Paris – the way the *platane* trees come into leaf in spring or seeing people sitting outside cafés following a winter hibernation – now filled me with resentment. For this? I left Mom and Dad for this bullshit? Paris hadn't caused my mother's death, but it played a role, I felt. And now my punishment was to live here, my purgatory for only-child guilt.

Then, in August, while on vacation, I was told Dad couldn't swallow and had pneumonia, and within a few days I found myself back in the States at the same hospital, on the same floor, two doors down from Mom's room, this time with Dad. The doctors gave a similar prognosis, citing again the magical thirty-six hours. And I chuckled, only because it felt as if I was cramming for another test in this condensed course on dying I'd taken this semester.

As with Mom, I found myself at the foot of Dad's bed. And again, I ran around it watching the oxygen drop, hoping the kids and Anaïs would arrive in time to see him. As with Mom, I rehashed old memories: how the first time I ever saw him cry was when he packed my U-Haul van for college or how he'd replay my peewee football games back to me in the car like the announcers did on Sundays, his grainy voice popping off the dashboard.

'Three minutes to play, the Bulldogs are driving. There's a handoff to von Sothen, who cuts to the outside, he's got one man to beat . . .' I apologised for hooking him in the foot when we were surf casting. I did my best imitation of Mr Langford. I rehashed old lines from *Blazing Saddles* and *Caddyshack*, films we'd watched countless times upstairs in the back bedroom. I reminded him he was the only one I'd swim to in the ocean as a child, the only one I ever trusted to breach the waves and not go under. And there in the hospital, as the sea of people in the ER rose up around us, I clung to Dad one last time as I had as a child. The oxygen, like the tide, soon dropped. He stopped breathing and, as the nurses came in to disconnect him, I stood there at his bed, alone now, an orphan.

I walked out dazed into the sticky Washington August heat, made only worse by being inside a hospital for three days. What shocked me was how people were buying stuff from food trucks and sitting on the lawn looking at their phones. Life, I assumed, had been put on pause this whole time, and I'd come out of the hospital to a giant 'mannequin challenge', everyone stiff and looking off into oblivion, waiting for me to give the sign that the film of life could start back up again.

♟ ♟ ♟

When you have another funeral for your other parent ninety days after the first, it's a lot easier. You call the same people, same church, same funeral home. You go with a cheaper casket this time. You make a better speech and you buy a summer suit from the same tailor who can't believe you're back again under similar circumstances. The estate lawyers know your name by now, and you understand what you're signing. The only thing that's different now is that, with both gone, it's clear there's no reason to call this place your home anymore. Because it's not.

We returned to Paris a few days after the funeral, because school was starting up again. And again, like clockwork, my poor neighbour Emily asked about vacation. When I told her what happened, she laughed out loud, because I had to be joking, right?

'No, I'm not kidding. He really died.' I, too, laughed because it did sound nuts and also because Emily's face, realising it was true, looked hilarious. Emily remains a good friend, but she's never asked me about vacation again.

My uncle Charlie would soon pass away, and just like that my America was amputated. Sure, there were cousins and godparents and summer camps and weddings and work, but after each trip, America faded more into a place to visit than a place to live. Expats are the biggest jihadists for single-payer health care. Once you have it, you're intolerant toward any other form of coverage or medical care. Anytime we vacation in the States, I take out an extra policy, as if we're travelling to some Third World country where one slip-up could cost you your house. I haven't paid one dollar for child care or health care or school, and yet still we struggle. How do Americans pull it off? I ask myself. How would I if we moved to the United States?

When we go to Washington, we make it a point to visit Mom's and Dad's graves, and we'll stay at the club where they were once members. We'll swim and see the old staff and sit in the Adirondack chairs where Mom and Dad drank their pinot grigios before dinner. But each year we do this, the memories of those experiences become fuzzier and things don't feel nostalgic so much as exotic.

Those parents and kids I see at the kiddie pool resemble my mother and me, sure. But I don't think she drank vodka and tonics in a sippy cup like the mothers there now. Nor did she drive those massive Cadillac Suburbans or Yukons. Was the TV always on in the restaurant? Were the waiters this eager and present? Did the supermarket fruit look this plastic? I can't remember. And these new names: Connor, Everett, Richmond and Hailey. Did I have friends with these names? Did everybody do aerobics at 6.45 am? Was there a mass shooting at a school each month? When did it become okay for leaf blowers to exist?

What also seemed foreign was how suddenly I understood everything so clearly. Conversations I didn't want to overhear came pouring over the booth as I sat in silence eating my childhood grilled cheese and sipping my Shirley Temple. I'm sure these conversations are just as insipid in France, but I don't have to listen to them there. I can block them and keep them muffled, because it's not my language. Not my people.

When I see old friends in Washington, I'll quickly home in on that nasal tone that the French say Americans have, and that I've always denied existed, until recently. During our chats, it'll dawn on me that if I add up all the years I've lived in France the sum comes close to half my life, and yet still I've never considered France home, probably because it's tough putting home behind you. You say goodbye to the ghosts. And when that pain of losing those you loved gradually eases, a sadness wells up, a sadness that strangely comes from relief. Pain, I realise, is a way of remembering everything in high-res detail and, without it, my parents dying and my childhood gradually feels smoothed over, cleaned up and replaceable. And for me, that's awfully sad.

If you go to Marseilles, you might see a series of sculptures sprinkled around the city by the artist Bruno Catalano titled *Les Voyageurs*. Each bronze statue features a man or woman walking with a bag, but half of their body is missing, as if a giant shark has taken out a chunk of their torso and legs. For some reason (and I don't know how) the statues manage to stand upright, the subject still looking forward, and whatever part is missing is replaced by whatever their present background holds. It could be a seaside view of the old port or a busy crowd at a bus stop, an ATM machine off to the left.

As an American living in France, I often feel like these statues. The chunk that is missing, your heart and your guts, is the home you've put behind you, filled in by a present that's colourful and in 3D, but that doesn't quite resemble you. That which does, the still-bronze fixed part, is your head and its memories, and the bag you hold, which (now that you're an expat) you know you can grab in a flash to claim another place as home, wherever that may be.

Sick of paying hundreds of dollars per month for years of storage, I eventually bit the bullet and shipped Mom and Dad's belongings by container across the ocean to Le Havre, the boat probably following the same route Mom's steamer took in the 1950s. They were then loaded onto a truck and driven down to our home in the Perche.

There, countless boxes and crates were dumped and sat another two years until, last summer, while Bibi and Otto were at summer camp, Anaïs and I opened them up one by one. Since there was no inventory, each box was a

Christmas gift full of memories that would pour out once the tape came undone and the top was opened. Otto got my grandfather's forty-eight-star American flag. The silverware, we polished and kept in the side cupboard for Christmas. Bibi and Anaïs took the furs. We put Dad's piano in the corner. And the framed photos of Uncle Charlie from his years at Yale went on the mantelpiece over the fireplace, next to Dad's Emmys.

What I most cherished, though, were Mom's paintings, some of them eight by ten feet. Each was different, but the style was the same: abstract and purple-headed, acrylic, and all painted during the sixties and seventies when I'd just been born, around the time I could walk and sit with her in her studio, high on turpentine. As a child, I didn't understand these works. Faces weren't in proportion; hands were stuck on torsos at the wrong spot. Mom, to me, couldn't draw well, so how could she be an artist? There were no classic landscapes, or sunrises. She'd painted the people she knew. Mr. Peele in Hatteras who drove Uncle Frank's boat. My friend Justin and me in our Speedos driving our big wheels. There were charcoals, too, from Paris, which she'd sketched while living there as a student: kids on horses in the *Tuileries*, parked bicycles near Les Halles, men selling books along the Seine, things I've seen millions of times in Paris and don't give two shits about, but that, to her, seemed exotic parts of a place far from home.

Now there's an opening in the works in Paris for Mom's paintings, which people call a *vernissage*, and which for years I fought, probably out of an odd desire to keep her all to myself and not to share her with the world. There's also a stack of French nationality papers I'm supposed to file, to become French as well as American, to accept once and for all, home is here. You could say that I'm finally accepting the pull part of France. I'm no longer fleeing my parents, because there's nobody to flee from. We're all here now, getting acclimated.

With all the new antiques and paintings and oriental rugs, our home in the Perche now resembles an upscale country inn more than a weekend house. Friends come out in the half-dozens if there's a Monday holiday. Some, on an hour's notice, jump on a train Friday evening and are here by dinner, knocking on the door, smiling and smelling of perfume. And while the night kicks into gear, and everyone's inside, I'll venture out to the garden and look back into the party from a distance. If you saw me there you'd see a strange man in a field peeing in the dark, but from my point of view the house looks like an illuminated doll's house, alive and breathing with life-sized figurines. The piano playing, the smokers, the laughers, the sixties paintings, the kids running through the tall adults chased by a wire-haired dog all look eerily familiar, taking me back to the America I most want to remember and refuse to let go of.

And there in the cold under those bright stars only the countryside can provide, I smile, because, once again, I can't hear or understand much of what's being said or why people are laughing or how it is I've even gotten here, for that matter, to this odd place I now call home. But just the way I sat on the staircase during those raucous nights in Georgetown on the outside looking in, I again find myself observing and analysing, translating and interpreting, learning and imitating, repeating and polishing, until the complicated, beautiful description of what it's like to live in this wacky *chez moi* is ready – ready to be written.

EPILOGUE

LIKE MANY PARISIAN FAMILIES, we occasionally rent our apartment out on Airbnb. It's not an easy process, but if you can power through the tedious chore of prepping your house and fielding calls from guests who forgot the code to your building, it does provide some disposable income. Which is handy for all those school year vacations that pop up in France every six weeks.

What many Parisian families do *not* do is rent out their apartment while they're not *en vacances* and when their kids are still in school, which is exactly what we did one year, forgetting that the Easter break for families in the south of France hits a week earlier than that in Paris. We realised this fun fact just days before our guests arrived, which sent us scrambling to find alternative lodging (on Airbnb, of course) in Montmartre, a hop, skip and another hop away from our own place in the Tenth Arrondissement.

It felt odd to pack up our clothes, the printer, plus the dog and cat, hairdryers and book bags, just to hoof it three metro stops west for a week. And sure, it was a bit bizarre to pass your own apartment in the morning on your way to school (now a twenty-minute schlep) and see the window of your bathroom fogged up from a stranger probably fucking in your shower.

But, in the end, the week turned out not half bad. It forced my family to break up a rut we didn't know we were in, and gave us the chance to see a part of Paris we hadn't had time to visit much. And it was during this impromptu staycation in Montmartre, dining out early with the kids at restaurants or ducking into a café for a beer midday or riding the bus (the bus?) and taking photos from the window of that bus, that I felt, for the first time in years, like an American in Paris. A tad curious, kind of stupid, and with much too much energy, not unlike the other Americans I saw in Montmartre that week, marching up single file to the Sacré-Coeur church, where they'd take in a breathtaking view of Paris while also being pickpocketed.

Some were backpackers on Snapchat, others were orthopaedic-shoed retirees carrying on about Sedona. And although they looked winded and footsore, each had an enthusiasm for Paris I hadn't felt in a long time. How could they not? Although it was now a bit Disney-fied, Montmartre had been the foothold for artists like Picasso and Modigliani and American expat writers like Langston Hughes, and its allure and romance were still potent. The streets were cobblestone and smoothed by time. Chickens turned on those sidewalk rotisseries. People leaned on flipped-over wine casks smacking back oysters and Muscadet.

I myself probably rounded out the cliché, a real-life Parisian writer in his pea coat and five-day-old scruff scribbling in his Moleskine what the world would never understand but which had to be written. Little did these tourists know, I was just as lost as them, and had they'd asked me in their *X-KUSAY MOI MESSSUR* French where the Moulin Rouge was, or in which restaurant Picasso traded his paintings for meals, I couldn't have helped. Because as a Parisian, I wouldn't be caught dead at any of them. Yet at the same time it burned me how I'd lost the innocence for this place. I'd strayed so far off the range and gone so deep into the recesses of French life that Montmartre now seemed Vegas to me.

Before I knew it, the week was over and I was back in my own Paris, the graffitied, kebab-standed, trash-strewn Tenth, feeling as if I'd just had an affair with another neighbourhood. And like any cheater, I immediately tried to mask my guilt by finding fault with my present home. 'Didn't it feel nice to just sit outside and hear that accordion play?' I'd suggest to Anaïs. I'd go on and on, harping about the cakes in the windows and the antique dealers, saying what a relief it was to not hear sirens or to not have my conscience weighed down as I consider the circumstances of the refugees we pass every day on the way to the metro.

But in my comparisons, I missed that our own Bohemian digs aren't all that much different from what Montmartre had been back in the day. Anaïs knows this, though, and she's keen enough to see how attached I actually am to our place. She even coined an expression – she claims she made it up, but it sounds too profound for that to be true – *'On critique bien, ce qu'on aime le mieux.'* ('We critique best what we love the most.')

Anaïs is right. I love my adoptive home; so much so, I feel I'm entitled now to flame it *à la Française*. Yet what I'm zinging isn't the French institutions themselves, but the Insta-gram version we Americans have imposed upon them.

Within every bestelling book about France by Americans (and the Brits are not much better), there's no doubt love, but it's always on our terms and one-way. We have this infatuation with keeping France a quaint and charming doll's house. If the vision isn't forged by Impressionist paintings, it's cantankerous civil servants who strike on a daily basis, or farmhouses basking in lavender fields, or a workplace where emails after 5pm aren't opened. If it's not warm baguettes and good wine, it's angelic kids in Bonpoint standing next to chic and severe mothers who don't get fat. According to such books, France isn't on the cusp of anything. It's in the preservation business, keeping civilisation alive.

When I moved here, all those years ago, I, too, was under the spell of a rose-coloured France. I had in my head that I'd be eating six-course dinners and vacationing three months a year with my French actress wife, while writing the next great American novel. The reality has proven quite differ-ent. But not in a bad way, just in a real-life, run-of-the-mill, everyday way that anybody who's working and raising kids, walking dogs, trying to get the Internet installed, paying a mortgage, and struggling to help with homework he him-self doesn't understand, can relate to.

For me, Paris is a mess, a confusing, roiling, weird place. If anything, it's America now with its Supreme T-shirt pop-up sales and cupcake parlors and hoverboards and Google stores that looks clean and vanilla and safe. Anytime I'm back in New York for work, it's me who takes on the clueless glaze of those Montmartre backpackers, wondering how the deli I used to buy forty-ounce beers at suddenly became an office building or why everyone feels obliged now to crank the AC in March. I'll question why Amtrak can't modernise, or how I missed the whole sippy-cup craze, and it's during these ruminations that I realise what the person across from me has pegged me for – everyday Eurotrash.

My life in France, I tell my friends, is a lot like going back in time to the United States in the 1970s, when the cities were rugged, cap gains were high, public schools were still doable, economic growth was minimal, people drank at lunch, and the national fabric and social net were intact, warts and all. When my American friends visit and I tell them this, I see there's a slight twinkle of new-found romance for France, based on a new set of criteria. There's also relief. France, the way I pitch it, isn't perfect at all. And because of that, it's accessible and, for the most part, English speaking, just like the rest of the world. Sure the Brie, Bordeaux and baguette thing still exists, but it doesn't define our life here. Plus those are things you can easily find in Manhattan or London or wherever.

What you can't find, though, or at least enter, is Notre Dame, whose ashes floated over our neighbourhood on a mid-April evening in 2019 and onto my hat while I came home from work. I loved Notre Dame because you could walk down our street, take a right on rue Faubourg Saint-Martin, which eventually became Rue Saint-Martin, which eventually leads you directly to Notre Dame's front. All our friends who visit start their Paris treks this way, and they always come back confirming I told the truth. It's a straight shot.

While my mother always described in detail the magic of the Christmas Midnight Mass she once attended there, I was smitten by Notre Dame's vending machines. Here you were inside one of the true wonders of the world, a place built in 1163 and which took almost two centuries to complete, and yet you could buy a candle or a souvenir like you were in a bus depot, then place it wherever you wanted for whoever you wanted. For me, Notre Dame didn't take itself too seriously, and that was its beauty. Beyond its fame and history, it was still a nuts-and-bolts working church. You could duck into a service without passing through too much security or take selfies in front of a chapel during that same service. The vending machines were there to raise money, of course, because Notre Dame always had a sort of 'let's make it through the end of the month' quality, which we know now is probably what led to the fire.

Other rare Parisian institutions include Doctor Benayoun, who comes to my house at midnight to give me a flu shot, raving about Miami and how we should go in on a condo together, or the professor I see when I walk my dog each night teaching French in his spare time from a whiteboard in the cold rain to Syrian refugees camped in our park. Nor could you find in any other city my aristo-rock-star father-in-law, who has two children my own children's ages and no qualms about asking me to babysit.

Enduring love, I've learned, is when you're smitten by something or someone for one reason, but you end up loyal to them for another.

Since our Montmartre staycation five years ago, we've made it a point each year to recreate it. We rent out our place during a work/school week, throw together the suitcases and dog food and book bags and staplers, and live for a few days somewhere else in Paris. We've done Bastille. We've done Le Marais. And this year we're venturing out to the no man's land of the Fifteenth. And, just as with our time in Montmartre, we'll admire the scenes or walk the Seine or check out a museum. Hell, we might even buy souvenirs. And in doing so, I'll once again feel like someone in the audience eating popcorn as he watches the stage production of '*Paris!*'

Invariably the clock will strike twelve and we'll return home, hoping the lucky family staying in our apartment had as much fun as we did. But judging from our Airbnb reviews, the compliments usually stop at the size of our loft. Most are a litany of masked disappointments. The bathroom towels were worn out, or they didn't exactly love the street, the neighbourhood was a bit too noisy and rough, a bit off the beaten trail. Our home in the Tenth wasn't the Paris they thought they'd be visiting, at least not the one featured in all those books they'd bought at the airport.

And in reading the feedback out loud in English to my cackling family and puzzled dog, I realise now how far from home an American can feel when he says in a perfectly accented French huff, '*Ooh là là... les Américains!*'

THANKS

THIS BOOK OWES ITS LIFE to my agent, the warrior queen Lindsay Edgecombe, who saw something in the burning coals of an idea and forged it into a shining sword. Without Lindsay's input and guidance, her meticulous notes and tough choices, her daily encouragement and military re-solve, none of this would have happened. Zero. Thanks also to those in my warrior queen's cavalry – the Levine Greenberg Rostan Agency, where Dan, Jim, Beth, Melissa, Ariel and Tim have been my extended family and friends long before they were my advocates. I heart them dearly.

Top billing is also in order for Mark Ellingham of Profile Books who cobbled and crafted, tinkered and tailored this bulky memoir and transformed it into a streamlined Eurostar. Working in the engine room was Nikky Twyman, my proofreader extraordinaire whose attention to detail and fluent French kept the text on track and passable for French customs.

Where would this book be without family? My mother Annie-Lou, Missouri, and my uncle Charlie and my grandmother Margaret, the Murdochs, including Molly and Mara, the von Sothens, Sue and Pete and Robert (all of whom at some point shared with me stories of our family and my mom). And *bien sûr*, there's the *bellest-belle-famille* a man could have: Hughes, Laure and Alain, Leïto,

Stéphane and Lazarre, Auntie Anne, Loreleï and John, Yolaine, Sachko, and Sibyl-Anna.

Bisous as well to my Percheron peeps: Lucien and Jocelyne, Sergei and Solange, Nathalie and Guillaume, Brigitte and Yann, Edwige, Alexandre and Amélie, our contractors, Ben and Arnaud, who put a roof over our head. Each of them gave me insight into the Perche and its people and each has confirmed to me in their own way why we've stayed.

Big ups to all of Bibi's and Otto's teachers, riding coaches, camp counsellors and Road's End Farm directors (I see you, Tom Woodman), soccer coaches, babysitters, assistantes maternelles, crèche handlers and *filles au pair* who looked after my children while I was probably off somewhere writing this book.

To May and Alvin, who've taken care of us and our home for ages. To my wonderful neighbours – Marie-Christine, Antoine and Virginie, and my fellow expat, Marc, at Bob's Bake Shop, who shared with me their stories about the neighbourhood and gave me good coffee and bagels and a place to write every morning.

To Otto's and Bibi's friends who've kept me young and brought me up to speed with French slang – Najl-Adams, Gabin, Jeanne, Lucien, Lou, Titouan – and to all of those who crashed Bibi's sweet sixteen. I know who you are.

To my dog, Bogart, and all my late pets – Socks, Dr Pepper, Teddy, Baron and Frisco –for their loyalty and companionship and being the best co-writers anyone could have.

To my wife, Anaïs (you're in the Dedication so stop complaining!), who's lived and breathed this book for almost three years now and amazingly still hasn't left me. And my two children, Bibi and Otto, the ones who begged me at night for more stories about 'when you were little' or 'Granny and Gramps', and who indirectly inspired me to write some of these chapters. All three of these musketeers have given me a life I never dreamed of having.

Finally, thanks to my dad, Dave, the one who misses out on all the glory (once again) and who finds himself (once again) at the bottom here, holding everyone up on his shoulders, much like those human pyramids we used to make at the beach – smiling and wincing 'Hurry up' while the rest of us looks forward and does one big group 'Cheese!' as the camera goes … 2 … 1 …click.